Six a day

A. L. Griffiths

ST. NICHOLAS SCHOOL

OLIVER & BOYD

Oliver & Boyd
Robert Stevenson House
1-3 Baxter's Place
Leith Walk
Edinburgh EH1 3BB

A Division of Longman Group UK Ltd

First published 1986
Second impression 1987

© A.L. Griffiths 1986
All rights reserved; no part of this publication
may be reproduced, stored in a retrieval system,
or transmitted in any form or by any means,
electronic, mechanical, photocopying, recording
or otherwise, without the prior written permission
of the Publishers

Set in 14pt Linotype Melior Roman

Designed and illustrated by Scorpion Pica
Produced by Longman Group (FE) Ltd
Printed in Hong Kong

ISBN 0 05 003923 7

Contents

NUMBER

	Exercises
The meaning of two-digit numbers	1-3
Order and counting to 100	4
Greater than – less than	5-8
Counting and the hundred chart	9
The meaning of three-digit numbers	10
Place value and the abacus	11-12
Writing three-digit numbers	13-15
Stressing place value	16
Rounding off numbers to the nearest 10	17
Rounding off numbers to the nearest 100	18
Roman numerals	19
Understanding addition	20
Addition and the number line	21
Understanding subtraction	22
Subtraction and the number line	23
Addition and subtraction practice	24-25
Order in addition	26-28
Grouping numbers in addition	29-30
Subtraction	31-32
Addition and subtraction	33-34
Odd and even numbers	36
A block graph	37
Addition of two-digit numbers	38
Subtraction of two-digit numbers	39
A thousand	41-43
Addition and subtraction – hundreds and tens	44-45
Place value	46-48
Understanding multiplication	49
Multiplication and repeated addition	50
Multiplication and the number line	51
Understanding division	52
Division and repeated subtraction	53
Multiplication and division relationship	54
Multiplication and division by 2	55-57
Multiplication and division by 4	59-63

More multiplication and division by 4	64
Multiplication and division by 10	65-67
Multiplication and division by 5	69-72
Multiplication and division by 3	74-77
Multiplication and division by 6	79-82
Is equal to – is not equal to	84
Mixed practice	85-88

MONEY

Counting money	89-92
Two and twenty pence coins	94
Coin collections	95-97
Changing pennies	99
Money problems	100
The fifty pence piece	101
The pound	102
Addition of money	104-107
Subtraction of money	109-112
More subtraction of money	114-115
Mixed practice	116-117
Multiplication of money	119-122
Division of money	124-127
Division problems with money	129
Mixed practice	130-132

LENGTH

The centimetre	134
The centimetre and the metre	135
The metre and the kilometre	136
Metres and centimetres – addition and subtraction	137-138
Mixed practice	139-141

MASS (WEIGHT)

The gram	143
The gram and the kilogram	144-148
More grams and kilograms	150

CAPACITY

The litre	151

CHECKING UP

152-172

MIXED REVISION

35, 40, 58, 63, 68, 73, 78, 83, 93, 98, 103, 108, 113, 118, 123, 128, 133, 142, 149

5 five

1 How many dots are there?

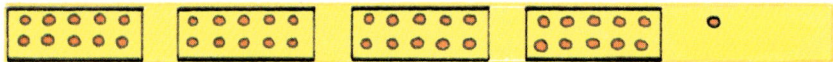

We can write the number in words:
> **forty-one**

or we can write the number in digits (figures):
> **41**

We can also show the number on an abacus.

How many shapes are there? Write each number in digits.

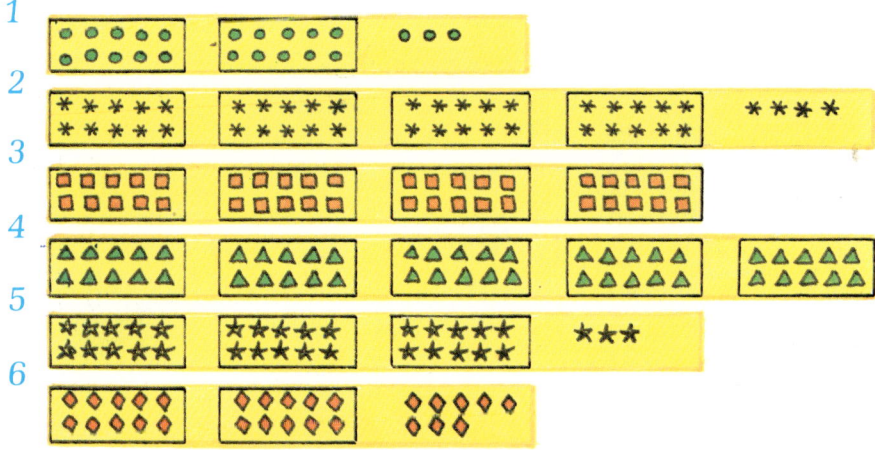

---

2 Write each of these numbers in digits, like this:

> **seventy-nine**   **79**

1 eighty   2 fifty-five

3 seventeen   4 forty-eight

5 forty-six   6 ninety-three

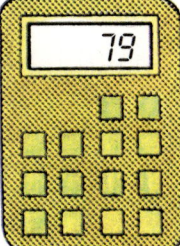

6 six

3 The abacus shows the number **fifty-two**.

Make simple abacus drawings to show these numbers.

1 ninety-six   2 nineteen
3 sixty-nine   4 seventy
5 eighty-three   6 fifty

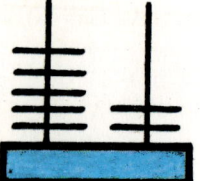

4 Look at the pattern of these numbers and then write out each row, putting in the missing numbers.

1 15, 16, 17, 18, ■, ■, ■, 22, 23
2 28, 26, 24, ■, ■, ■, 16, 14, 12
3 6, 8, ■, ■, ■, 16, 18, 20, 22
4 87, 88, ■, ■, ■, 92, 93, 94, 95
5 ■, ■, ■, 31, 32, 33, 34, 35, 36
6 20, 30, 40, ■, ■, ■, 80, 90, 100

5

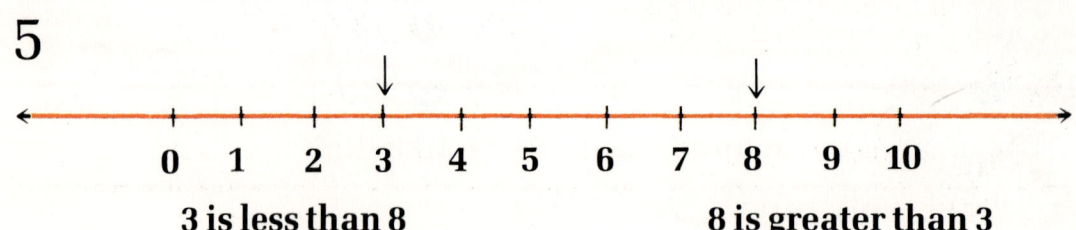

3 is less than 8   8 is greater than 3

3 < 8   8 > 3

Write < or > in place of each ●.

1 49 ● 94   2 40 ● 14   3 eighty ● eighteen
   94 ● 49   14 ● 40   eighteen ● eighty

4 87 ● 78   5 38 ● 83   6 ten tens ● 90
   78 ● 87   83 ● 38   90 ● ten tens

7 seven

6 1 Which of these numbers is greater than thirty-five and less than sixty?

| 29 | 17 | 33 | 86 | 49 | 94 | 61 |

2 Which of these numbers is forty more than forty-one?

| 18 | 48 | 84 | 14 | 41 | 81 | 80 |

3 Name the number which is 1 less than 90.

4 Name the number which is one more than fifty-nine.

5 What number is greater than seventy-nine and less than eighty-one?

6 What number is ten more than 63?

7 Write < or > in place of each ●.
1 598 ● 589
2 730 ● 370
3 521 ● 721
4 508 ● 580
5 499 ● 500
6 706 ● 607

8 Use the correct sign (<, > or =) in place of each ●.

If you really understand numbers, you will find these very easy.

1 70 + 9 ● 90 + 7
2 93 ● 30 + 9
3 700 + 40 + 0 ● 700 + 0 + 4
4 90 + 7 ● 7 + 90
5 100 + 80 + 7 ● 817
6 700 + 60 + 5 ● 657

9

1	2	3	4	5	6	7	8	9	10
11	12	13	14	15	16	17	18	19	20
21	22	23	24	25	26	27	28	29	30
31	32	33	34	35	36	37	38	39	40
41	42	43	44	45	46	47	48	49	50
51	52	53	54	55	56	57	58	59	60
61	62	63	64	65	66	67	68	69	70
71	72	73	74	75	76	77	78	79	80
81	82	83	84	85	86	87	88	89	90
91	92	93	94	95	96	97	98	99	100

Use the chart to help you with these questions.

1 What number is twenty more than sixty?

Write the answer in digits.

2 What number is fifteen more than eighty?

Write the answer in digits.

3 What number is twenty-three more than seventy?

Write the answer in digits.

4 What number is 30 less than 70? Write the answer in words.

5 What number is 25 less than 45? Write the answer in words.

6 What number is 20 more than seventy-six?

Write the answer in words.

9 nine

10 This picture shows 163 small cubes.

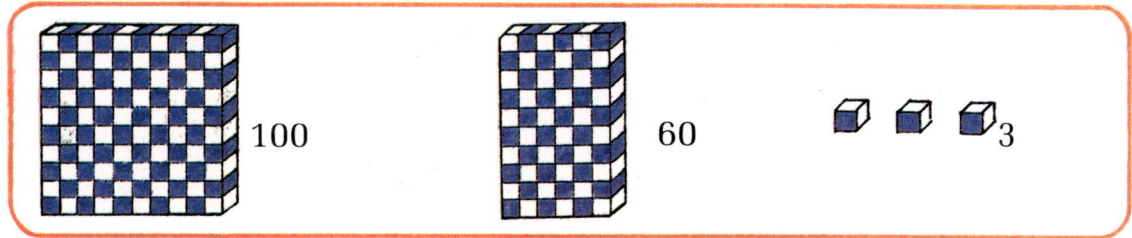

How many small cubes are shown in each of these pictures?

1

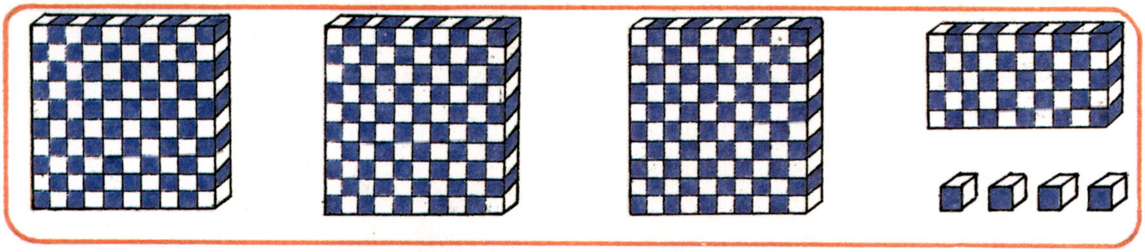

2

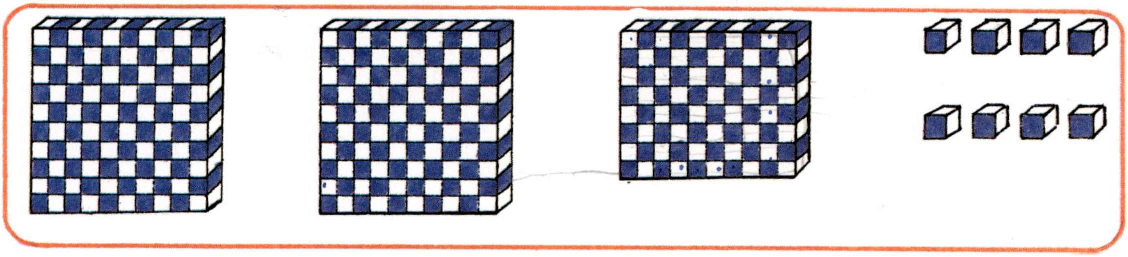

3

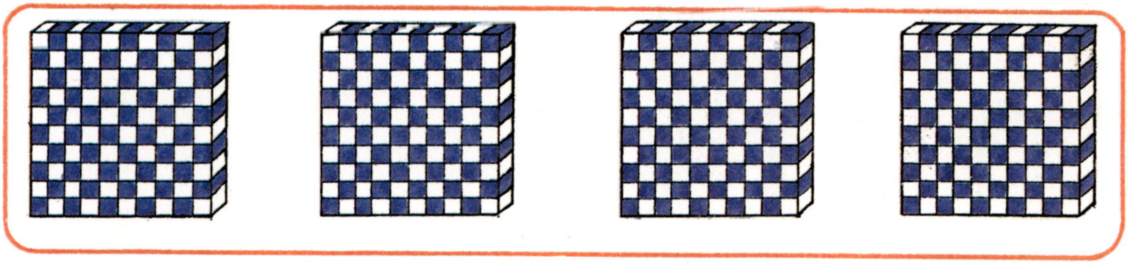

4

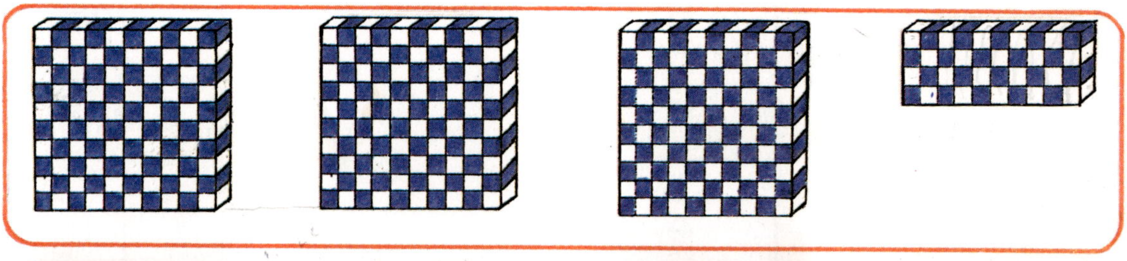

5 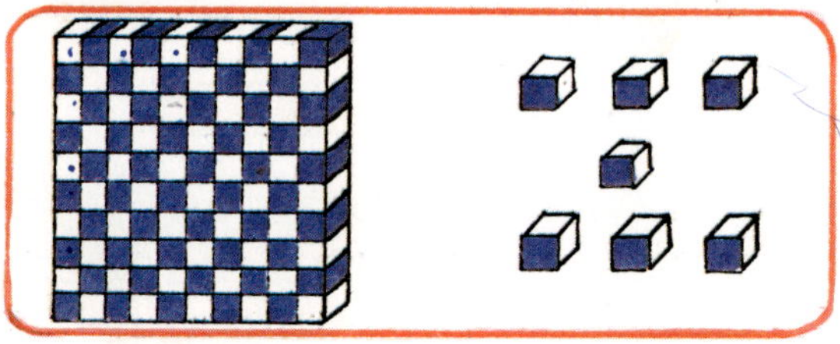 6

10 ten

11 There are **two hundred and thirty-four** rods shown in this picture.

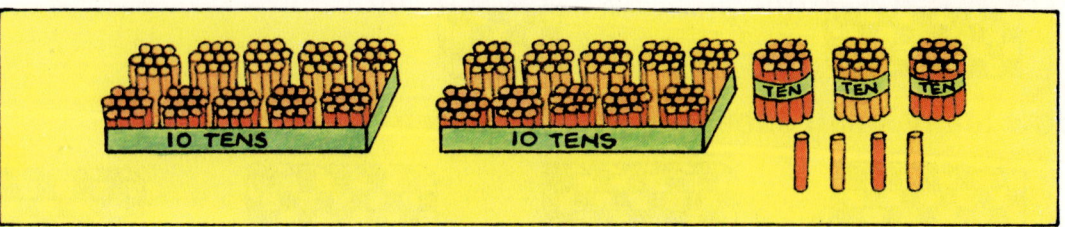

The abacus shows this number too.

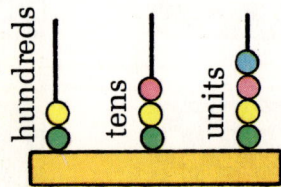

Each abacus below shows a different number. Count the number of hundreds, tens and units. Now write the whole number in words, then in digits.

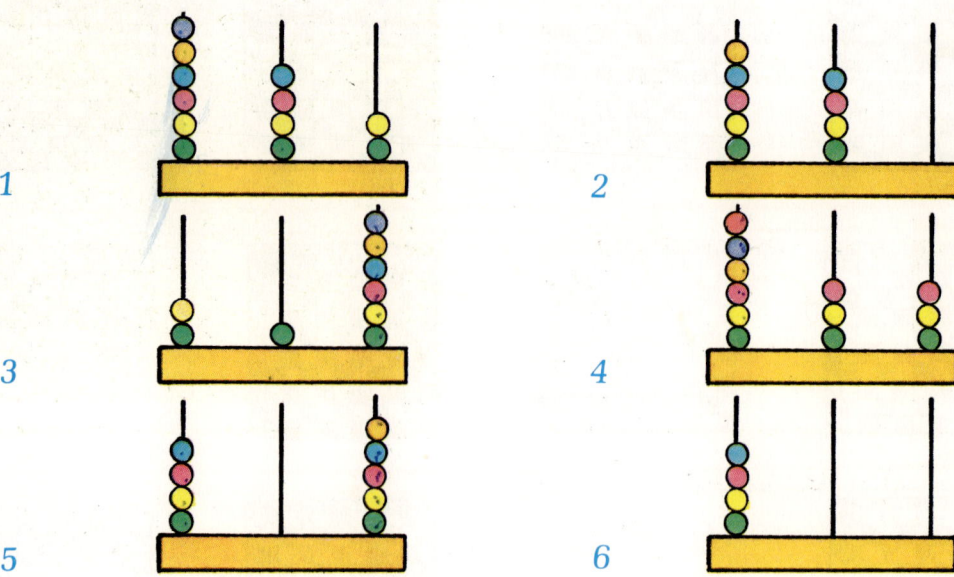

1   2

3   4

5   6

11 eleven

12 Draw a simple abacus to show each of these numbers.

1 520   2 716
3 76   4 900
5 504   6 375

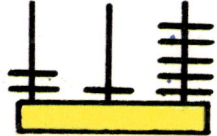

13 How many stamps are there of each price?
Write each number in digits.

1 11p two sheets of 100, five rows of 10 and two single stamps.

2 12p four sheets of 100, nine rows of 10 and six single stamps.

3 13p nine sheets of 100 and two single stamps.

4 14p seven sheets of 100 and five rows of 10.

5 15p six sheets of 100.

6 16p eight sheets of 100, one row of ten and three single stamps.

14 Write these numbers in digits.

1 nine hundred and six   2 five hundred and fifteen
3 four hundred and seventy-four   4 seven hundred
5 four hundred and forty   6 two hundred and eleven

12 twelve

15 How many picture stickers do you have altogether if you have:
1   178 and get 100 more?
2   293 and get 10 more?
3   399 and get 1 more?
4   703 and give away 10?
5   680 and give away 100?
6   460 and give away 1?

---

16   1 Look at these numbers carefully.   786   678   768
Now write them out in order of size from the least to the greatest.

2 Write these numbers out in order of size from the greatest to the least.   546   645   564   654

3 **674 = 600 + 70 + 4**
Now write this equation in the same way.
983 = ☐ + △ + ◇

4 In 497 the **7** means 7 units.
What does the **7** mean in 763?

5 If I have 3 packs of 100 tickets,
8 packs of 10 and 7 single tickets,
how many tickets have I altogether?

6 How many dots are there in this picture? (Remember it is easier and quicker to count in tens.)

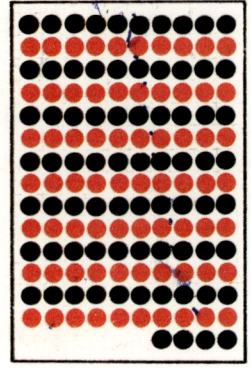

13 thirteen

17 Sometimes we only need to know **about** how many.

Round numbers are easier to remember and to use.

From Guildford to London is 48 kilometres.
We sometimes say it is **about 50 kilometres**.

A number ending in 5 is halfway between two tens and is always rounded off to the ten above.

25 rounded off to the nearest ten is 30.

How many stars are there in each of these pictures?
Round off the numbers to the nearest ten.

14 fourteen

18 There are 429 pupils in Grove School.

When the number is **rounded off** to the nearest hundred, we say that there are 400 pupils.

When a number ends in 50 we always round it off to the hundred above: **350 would be rounded off to 400**.

1 Round off 473 to the nearest ten.
2 Round off 239 to the nearest ten.
3 Round off 473 to the nearest hundred.
4 Round off 239 to the nearest hundred.
5 Round off 451 to the nearest hundred.
6 Round off 809 to the nearest hundred.

---

19 Another way to name numbers is to use **Roman numerals**.

I = 1   VII = 5 + 1 + 1
II = 1 + 1   VIII = 5 + 1 + 1 + 1
III = 1 + 1 + 1 IX = 10 − 1
IV = 5 − 1   X = 10
V = 5   XI = 10 + 1
VI = 5 + 1   XII = 10 + 1 + 1

Notice that the Romans wrote **IV (5 − 1)** for 4 and **IX (10 − 1)** for 9.

To find the Roman number we have to add the numerals, like this: XVI = X + V + I = 10 + 5 + 1 = 16

Now write these in our own numerals.

1 XV   2 XVI   3 XIV
4 XX   5 XIX   6 XXXI

15 fifteen

20 Look at each picture carefully, then find the number you can put in place of each ■. Here is an example.

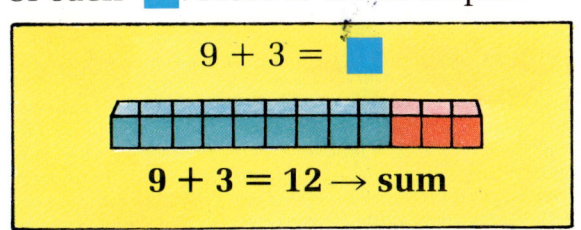

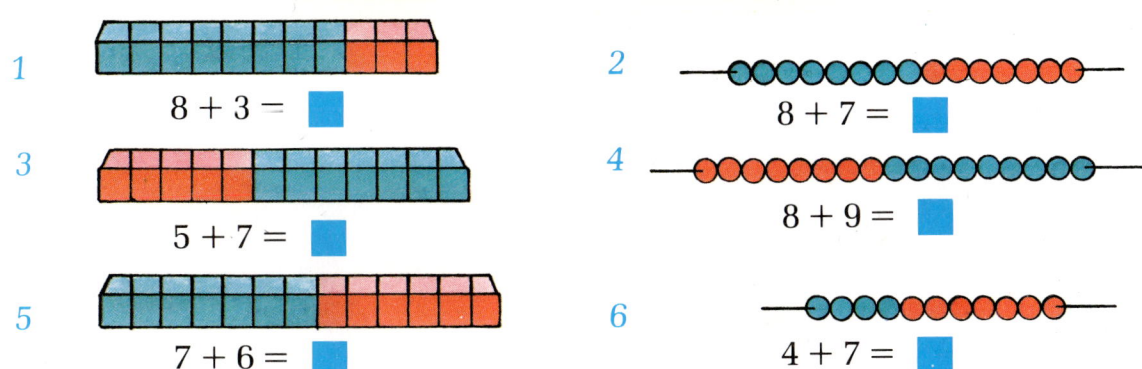

1. 8 + 3 = ■
2. 8 + 7 = ■
3. 5 + 7 = ■
4. 8 + 9 = ■
5. 7 + 6 = ■
6. 4 + 7 = ■

21

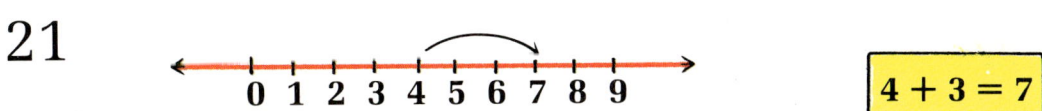

4 + 3 = 7

Write an equation like the one above for each of these number lines.

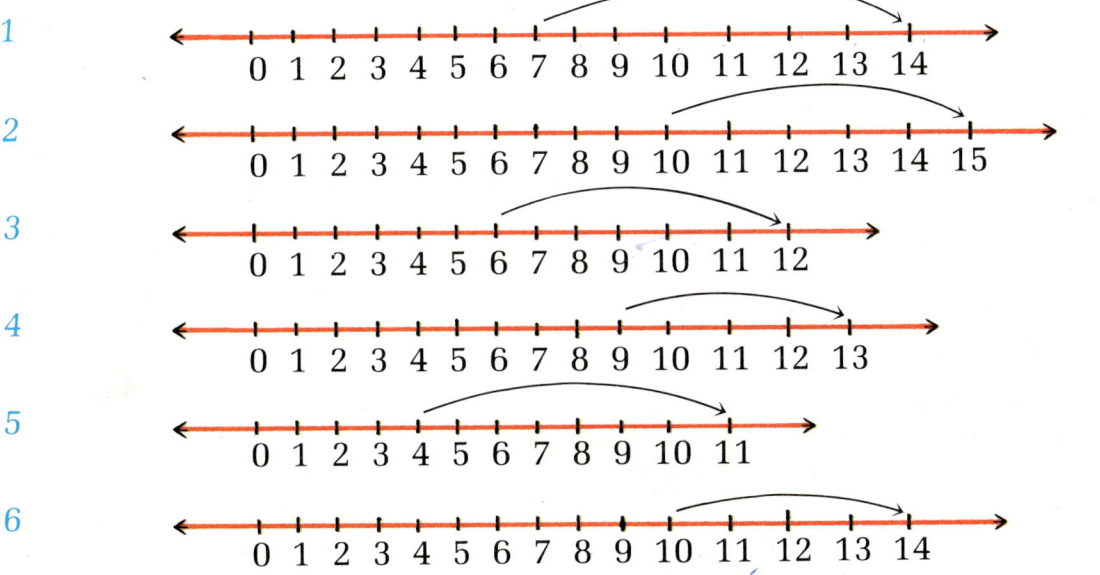

16 sixteen

22 Look at each picture carefully, then find the number you can put in place of each ■, like this:

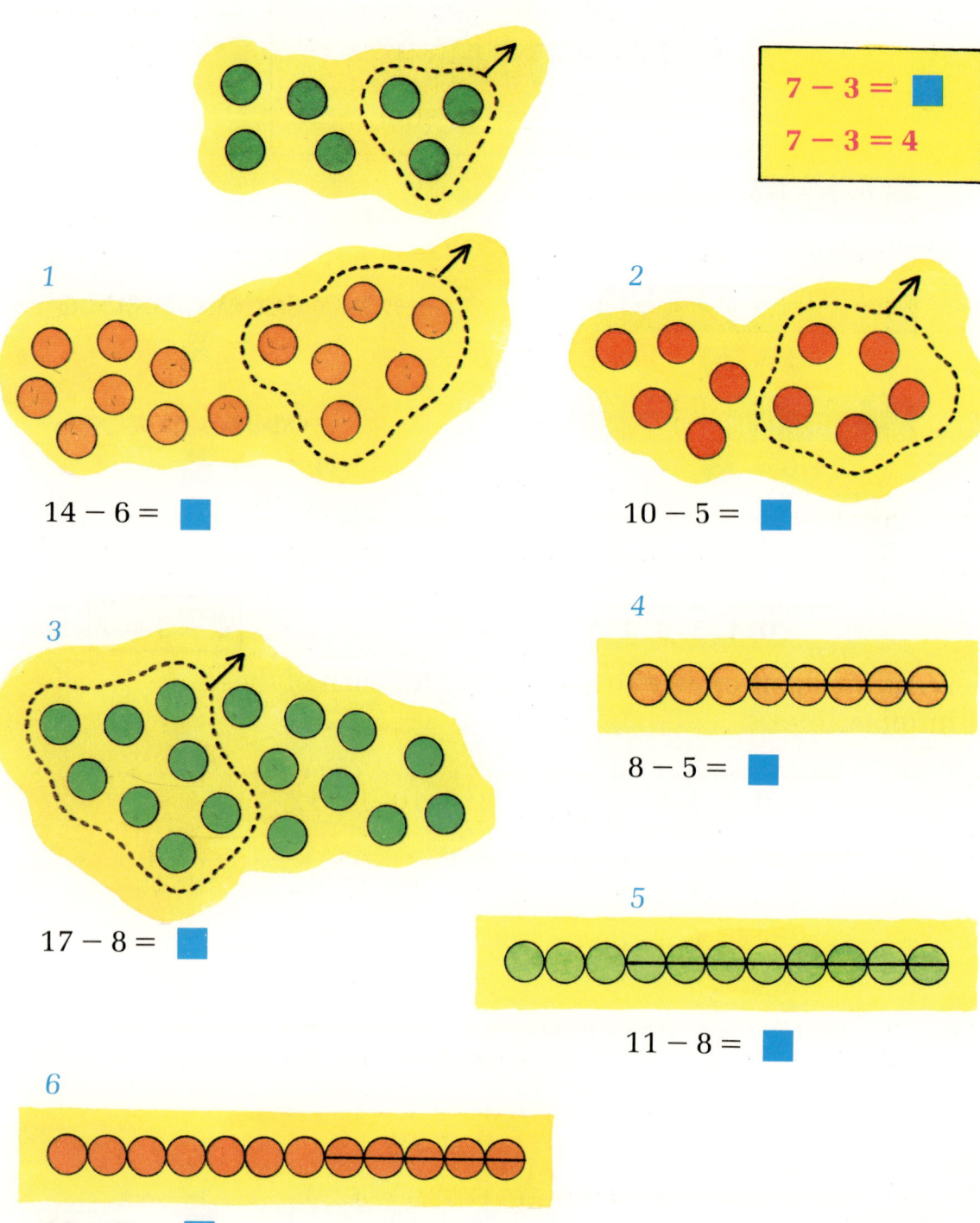

7 − 3 = ■
7 − 3 = 4

1
14 − 6 = ■

2
10 − 5 = ■

3
17 − 8 = ■

4
8 − 5 = ■

5
11 − 8 = ■

6
12 − 5 = ■

17 seventeen
23

$$13 - 5 = 8$$

Write an equation like the one above for each of these number lines.

1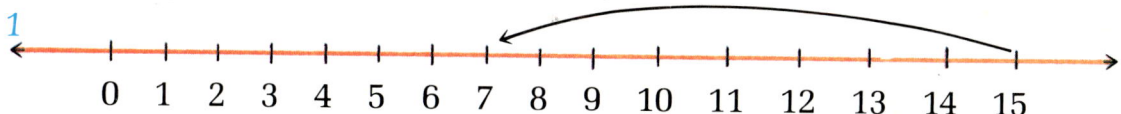

2

3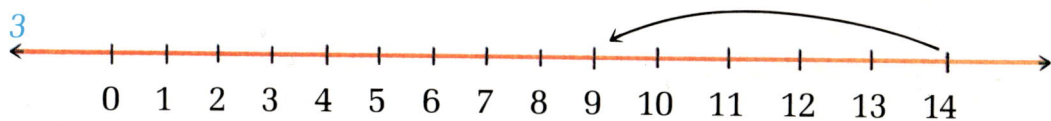

4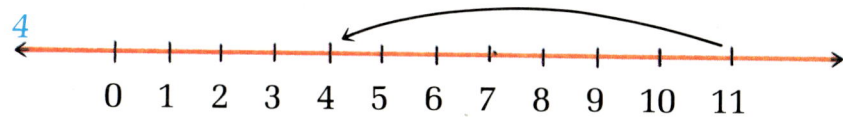

5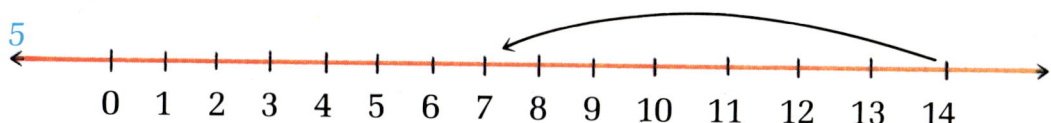

6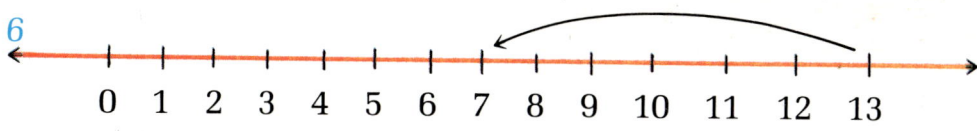

18 eighteen

24 What number can you put in place of each ■?

1 $6 + \square = 13$
2 $\square + 8 = 13$
3 $\square + 9 = 18$
4 $\square + 7 = 14$

5 $\square$
   $\underline{+\ 6}$
   $1\ 5$

6 6
   $\underline{+\ \square}$
   $1\ 4$

25 What number can you put in place of each ■?

1 $13 - \square = 6$
2 $13 - \square = 4$
3 $\square - 5 = 8$
4 $18 - 9 = \square$

5 $\square\square$
   $\underline{-\ 7}$
   4

6 $1\ 5$
   $\underline{-\ \square}$
   8

26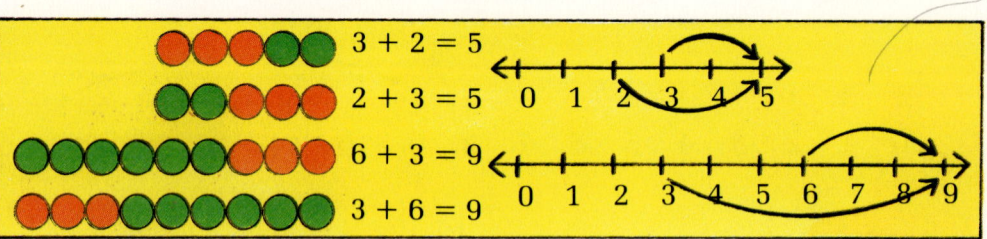

Study the additions in the box above.

Now solve these equations by finding the number you can put in place of each ■ or letter.

1 $4 + 9 = 9 + \square$
2 $6 + 7 = 7 + \boxed{x}$
3 $9 + 7 = \boxed{a} + 9$
4 $9 + \boxed{n} = 4 + 9$
5 $\square + 6 = 6 + 5$
6 $3 + 9 = 9 + \square$

19 nineteen

27 Solve these equations by finding the number you can put in place of each ■.

1 $5 + 9 = 8 + \square$
2 $4 + 9 = 8 + \square$
3 $2 + 5 = 4 + \square$
4 $5 + 7 = 7 + \square$
5 $4 + 6 = 6 + \square$
6 $6 + 6 = 8 + \square$

28 Solve these equations.

1 $5 + 8 = 7 + \square$
2 $7 + 8 = 8 + \square$
3 $6 + 7 = \square + 6$
4 $3 + 8 = 6 + \square$
5 $2 + 9 = 8 + \square$
6 $4 + 7 = 9 + \square$

29 $(3 + 2) + 4 = 9$
        $3 + (2 + 4) = 9$

In addition, the way in which we group numbers does not change the sum.

Use the useful law above when you work out these additions.

1 $4 + 6 + 8 = \square$
2 $5 + 17 + 3 + 0 = \square$
3 $9 + 7 + 3 = \square$
4 $25 + 5 + 5 + 7 = \square$
5 $6 + 4 + 8 = \square$
6 $9 + 16 + 4 = \square$

30 We now know that we can add numbers in any order we wish. It is sometimes helpful to look for pairs of numbers that add up to ten. Try these.

1 $6 + 9 + 4$
2 $8 + 4 + 5 + 2$
3 $5 + 5 + 6 + 4$
4 $6 + 3 + 4 + 7$
5 $4 + 7 + 3 + 2$
6 $9 + 6 + 1 + 4$

=SPEED=
Try to find the answers to these in 30 seconds.

31 Solve these equations.

1 $6 - 5 = 8 - \square$
2 $16 - 3 - 7 = \square$
3 $7 - 4 = 9 - \square$
4 $19 - 5 - 8 = \square$
5 $10 - 5 = 14 - \square$
6 $28 - 9 - 1 - 7 - 3 = \square$

20 twenty

32 Complete each number sentence.

1 9 is ▇ less than 18.   2 14 is ▇ more than 7.
3 7 is ▇ less than 15.   4 17 is ▇ more than 9.
5 5 is ▇ less than 11.   6 15 is ▇ more than 6.

33

1 Add eleven, nine and three.
2 What is the sum of 7, 6 and 4?
3 How many are fourteen and six?
4 7 plus 9 plus 3.
5 Find the total of 7, 6 and 4.
6 Martin had sixteen conkers left after giving four to his brother. How many did he have at first?

34

1 What number must you add to 7 to make 13?
2 Take 11 from 20.
3 What number is 5 less than 21?
4 What is the difference between 6 and 60?
5 Subtract 5 from 18.
6 A coin album can hold 48 coins. Ali has put in 18. How many more can the album hold?

21 twenty-one

35

1 Write five hundred and eight in digits.
2 What is the difference between 9 and 19?
3 Find the total of 6, 7 and 4.
4 What number is 5 less than the sum of 4 and 7?
5

I am thinking of a number. If I subtract 3 and then 4 from the number, I get 8. What is the number?

6 Since 9 − 6 = 3, we know that 49 − 6 = ▪.

---

36 Use the numbers on the left to help you work out the answers to these.

1 What is the next even number greater than 10?
2 Write the odd number which is greater than 13 and less than 17.
3 What is the sum of the even numbers which are less than 5?
4 Find the sum of all the odd numbers less than 4 and take it from 5.
5 How many odd numbers are there between 2 and 10?
6 Add three odd numbers. Is the answer odd or even?

odd   odd   odd   ?
▪ + ▪ + ▪ = ▪

22 twenty-two

37

Pets

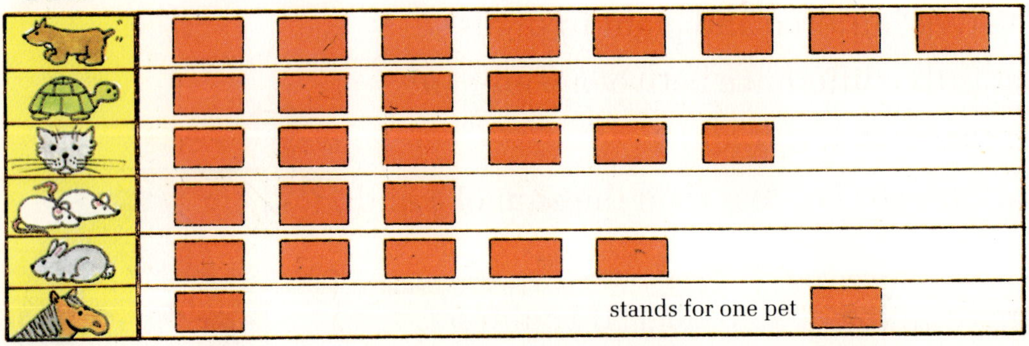

stands for one pet

This block graph shows the pets belonging to the children in Class I.

1 Which is the most popular pet?
2 How many more dogs are there than tortoises?
3 How many cats and dogs are there altogether?
4 How many more rabbits and mice are there than tortoises?
5 How many more dogs are there than tortoises and mice together?
6 What is the total number of pets?

38

1 Add forty and fifty.
2 Find the total of twenty, forty and ten.
3 What is the sum of sixty and twenty-five?
4 Add eighty-six and eleven.
5 24 + 40 + 2 = ▧
6 34 + 65 = ▧

23 twenty-three

39

1 Take thirty from eighty.
2 How many more is ninety than seventy-five?
3 Adam had a hundred marbles. He gave away thirty. How many had he left?
4 Take thirty-three from sixty-three.
5 78 − 40 − 5 =
6 39 − 17 =

40

1 Write in words the number shown on the abacus.
2 Solve this equation by finding the number which can be put in place of $\boxed{n}$.
$$7 + 16 = \boxed{n} + 7$$
3 What is the sum of the even numbers between 3 and 7?
4 Work out the missing number in this addition.

```
     ☐
     6
   + 7
   ───
   1 9
```

5 How many pencils are there? Write the number in digits.
6 Emma bought a box of 24 chocolate wafers. She ate 7 and gave away 5. How many were left in the box?

24 twenty-four

41
You may use the pictures on the right to help
you with the questions in Exercises 41, 42, and 43.

How many must be added to each of these numbers to
make a thousand? Write each answer in digits.
1 700   2 100   3 990
4 850   5 650   6 440

42
How many less than a thousand is each of these numbers?
Write each answer in digits.
1 960   2 550   3 290
4 370   5 740   6 180

43
Write these numbers in digits.
1 half a thousand
2 a quarter of a thousand
3 a hundred more than a thousand
4 a tenth of a thousand
5 fifty less than a thousand
6 ten less than a thousand

44 Use your calculator to check your answers.
1 Add 350 and 50.
2 Find the total of 150, 200 and 250.
3 How many more is 500 than 50?
4 Take 399 from 500.
5 Subtract 90 from 900.
6 Find the sum of 260, 40 and 500.

25 twenty-five

45 Can you see how these numbers grow?
Name the missing numbers.

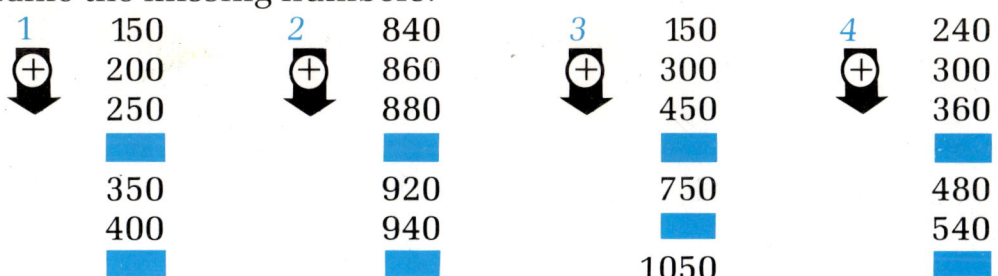

Can you see how these numbers decrease?
Write down the missing numbers.

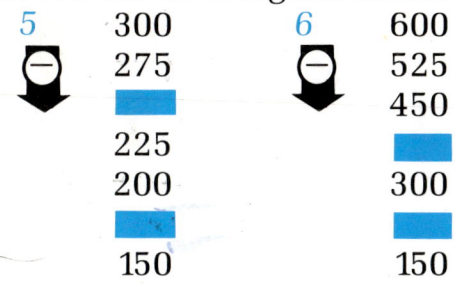

46

> < means **is less than**   > means **is greater than**.
> 63 **is less than** 79 can be written 63 < 79.
> 79 **is greater than** 63 can be written 79 > 63.

Copy, and put > or < in place of each ●, like this:
63 ● 69 is written 63 < 69.

1 49 ● 94   2 79 ● 97
3 90 ● 19   4 110 ● 101
5 111 ● 100   6 110 ● 111

47 Put > or < in place of each ●.
1 1001 ● 1100   2 1011 ● 1002
3 1011 ● 1110   4 1111 ● 1101
5 1111 ● 1200   6 1011 ● 1111

48 1 Add 1 to 909.   2 Add 1 to 299.
3 Subtract 1 from 990.   4 Subtract 1 from 799.
5 Add 10 to 705.   6 Subtract 10 from 403.

26 twenty-six

49 I can write two multiplication sentences for these drawings.

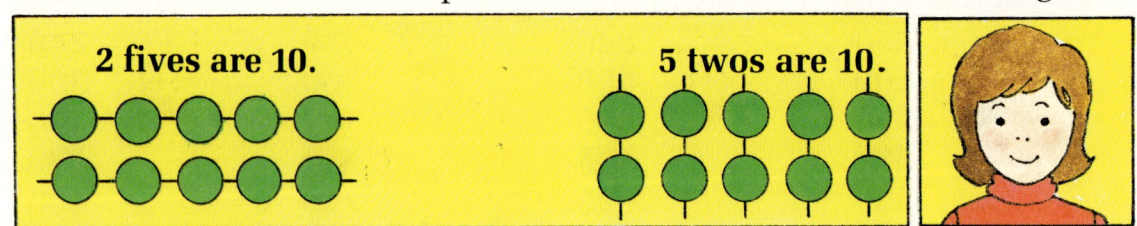

Complete these number sentences.

1 3 fours are ◼.   2 4 threes are ◼.   3 6 threes are ◼.

4 3 sixes are 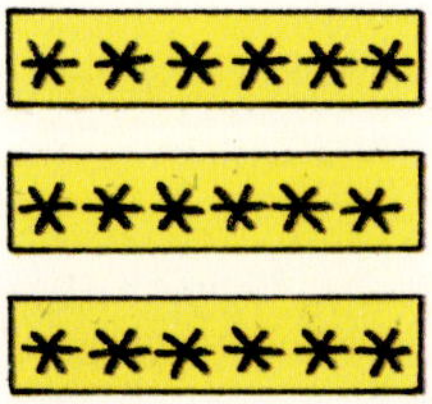 ◼.   5 3 fives are ◼.   6 2 sevens are ◼.
                      5 threes are ◼.   7 twos are ◼.

50 Look at this example.

$$2 + 2 + 2 + 2 + 2 + 2 = 6 \times 2 = 12$$

Now write a multiplication equation for each of these additions.
1 5 + 5 + 5 + 5 + 5 + 5
2 10 + 10 + 10 + 10 + 10 + 10 + 10 + 10 + 10
3 2 + 2 + 2 + 2 + 2 + 2 + 2 + 2 + 2 + 2
4 4 + 4 + 4 + 4 + 4 + 4 + 4 + 4 + 4
5 3 + 3 + 3 + 3 + 3
6 6 + 6 + 6 + 6 + 6 + 6 + 6

27 twenty-seven

51

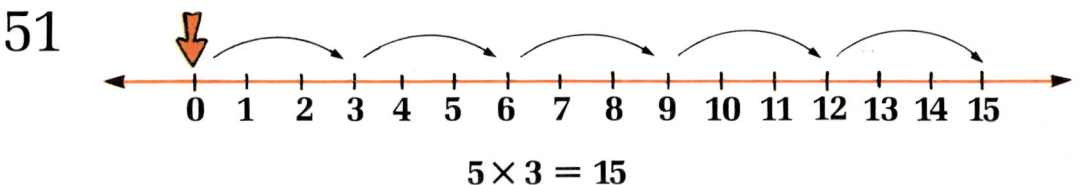

$5 \times 3 = 15$

Look at the example above, then write a multiplication equation for each of these number lines.

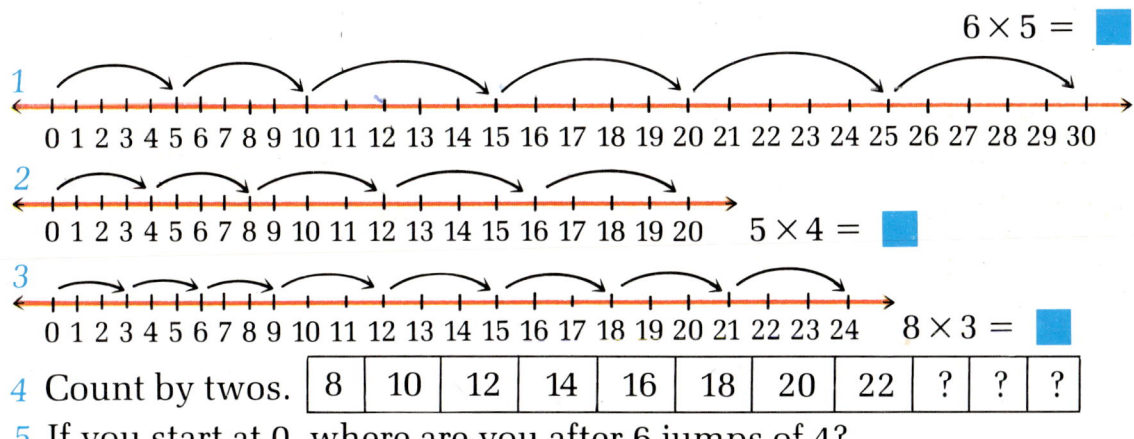

4 Count by twos. | 8 | 10 | 12 | 14 | 16 | 18 | 20 | 22 | ? | ? | ? |

5 If you start at 0, where are you after 6 jumps of 4?
6 If you start at 0, where are you after 4 jumps of 6?

52

We write **8 ÷ 4 = 2**.
We say **8 divided by 4 equals 2**.

Look at this division:

$12 \div 4 = $ ▇.

Think: How many fours equal 12?

$12 \div 4 = 3$

28 twenty-eight

Work out these divisions by counting the number of jumps on a number line.

1 18 ÷ 3 = ⬛   *2* 18 ÷ 2 = ⬛
3 28 ÷ 4 = ⬛   *4* 25 ÷ 5 = ⬛
5 20 ÷ 4 = ⬛   *6* 16 ÷ 2 = ⬛

53

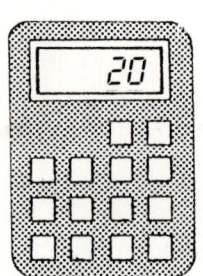

$$\begin{array}{c}20\\-4\\\hline 16\end{array} \nearrow \begin{array}{c}16\\-4\\\hline 12\end{array} \nearrow \begin{array}{c}12\\-4\\\hline 8\end{array} \nearrow \begin{array}{c}8\\-4\\\hline 4\end{array} \nearrow \begin{array}{c}4\\-4\\\hline 0\end{array}$$

20 ÷ 4 = 5

Write a division equation like the one above for each of these.

1
$\begin{array}{c}60\\-10\\\hline 50\end{array}$ $\begin{array}{c}50\\-10\\\hline 40\end{array}$ $\begin{array}{c}40\\-10\\\hline 30\end{array}$ $\begin{array}{c}30\\-10\\\hline 20\end{array}$ $\begin{array}{c}20\\-10\\\hline 10\end{array}$ $\begin{array}{c}10\\-10\\\hline 0\end{array}$ 60 ÷ 10 = ⬛

2
$\begin{array}{c}15\\-3\\\hline 12\end{array}$ $\begin{array}{c}12\\-3\\\hline 9\end{array}$ $\begin{array}{c}9\\-3\\\hline 6\end{array}$ $\begin{array}{c}6\\-3\\\hline 3\end{array}$ $\begin{array}{c}3\\-3\\\hline 0\end{array}$ 15 ÷ 3 = ⬛

3
$\begin{array}{c}10\\-2\\\hline 8\end{array}$ $\begin{array}{c}8\\-2\\\hline 6\end{array}$ $\begin{array}{c}6\\-2\\\hline 4\end{array}$ $\begin{array}{c}4\\-2\\\hline 2\end{array}$ $\begin{array}{c}2\\-2\\\hline 0\end{array}$ 10 ÷ 2 = ⬛

4
$\begin{array}{c}25\\-5\\\hline 20\end{array}$ $\begin{array}{c}20\\-5\\\hline 15\end{array}$ $\begin{array}{c}15\\-5\\\hline 10\end{array}$ $\begin{array}{c}10\\-5\\\hline 5\end{array}$ $\begin{array}{c}5\\-5\\\hline 0\end{array}$ 25 ÷ 5 = ⬛

5 Use subtraction to find the missing numeral.
    24 ÷ 4 = ⬛
6 Work out this division by counting in threes from 15 back to 0. 15, 12 . . .
    15 ÷ 3 = ⬛

29 twenty-nine

54 Look at this example.

> 6 fives are in 30.   6 fives = 30
> $30 \div 5 = 6 \rightarrow 6 \times 5 = 30$

Now write out these equations in full.

1 $20 \div 4 = \square \rightarrow \square \times 4 = 20$ 2 $24 \div 6 = \square \rightarrow \square \times 6 = 24$
3 $25 \div 5 = \square \rightarrow \square \times 5 = 25$ 4 $40 \div 10 = \square \rightarrow \square \times 10 = 40$
5 $12 \div 2 = \square \rightarrow \square \times 2 = 12$ 6 $24 \div 3 = \square \rightarrow \square \times 3 = 24$

---

55   When two numbers are multiplied the answer is called the **product**.
$3 \times 4 = 12$
The 12 is the product.

1 How many are eight twos?
2 What is the product of 9 and 2?
3 I am thinking of a number. 7 is half the number. What is the number?
4 Usha had 20 balloons. She gave 2 to each of the friends who came to her birthday party. If all the balloons were given away, how many friends were at the party?
5 How many twos are there in 40?
6 There are 16 children in a swimming club. There are the same number of boys as girls. How many of each are there?

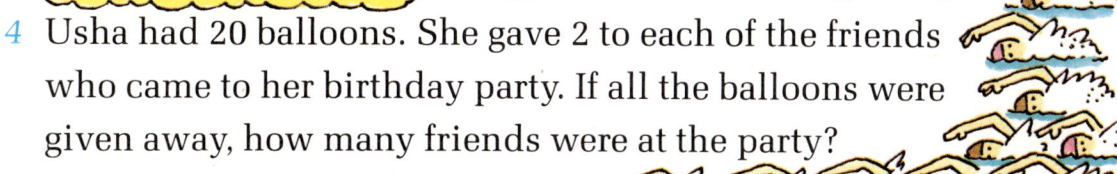

56

1 What is half of 18?
2 David has 24 marbles. He has the same number in each hand. How many are in each hand?

30 thirty

3 Adam and Karen each have 11 crayons. How many do they have altogether?
4 The sum of two numbers is the same as their product. What are the numbers?
5 2 × 0 = ▣   0 × 2 = ▣   6 ▣ ÷ 2 = 20

57 Look at these examples carefully.
70 multiplied by 2

Think: 7 tens multiplied by 2 = 14 tens = 140.

80 divided by 2

Think: 8 tens divided by 2 = 4 tens = 40.

Now try these.

1 30 × 2 = ▣   2 120 divided by 2
3 90 multiplied by 2   4 half of 60 = ▣
5 50 × 2 = ▣   6 140 ÷ 2 = ▣

58

1 Write seven hundred and seven in digits.
2 Lisa has 555 stamps in one album and 105 in her other album. How many stamps has she altogether?
3 What number is twice as great as the total of 7, 10 and 13?
4 A number minus 8 equals 7. What is the number?
5 Write the correct sign (<, = or >) in place of ●.   6 × 0 ● 5 × 1
6 Rex and Rover are the same weight. How heavy is Rex?

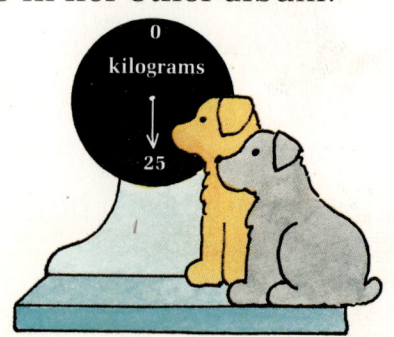

31 thirty-one

59

1 How many are there in 4 rows of 4?
2 What is the product of 6 and 4?
3 A quarter of a number is 20. What is the number?
4 How many fours are there in twenty?
5 28 ÷ 4 = ▊
6 How many tickets are needed to give 10 children 4 tickets each?

60

1 What is one quarter of 24?
2 Divide 32 by 4.
3 How many fours are there in thirty-six?
4 Mrs May bought four boxes of apples. How many apples did she have?
5 What is 4 times 7?
6 If you multiply me by 4, you get 36. Who am I?

61

Think: 90 ÷ 3 = 9 tens ÷ 3 = 3 tens = 30.

Now try these.

1 80 ÷ 4 = ▊   2 30 x 4 = ▊   3 $\frac{1}{4}$ of 160 = ▊
4 4 times 60 equals ▊   5 200 ÷ 4 = ▊   6 forty multiplied by four

---

62

15 ÷ 4 = ▊

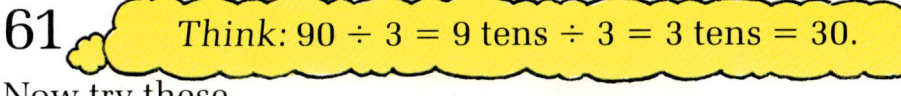

There are 3 fours in 15 and 3 left over.
15 ÷ 4 = 3 **remainder** 3

32 thirty-two

1 What is the remainder when 19 is divided by 5?
2 How many are left over after an equal number of these marbles are put in each tin?

3 What is the remainder when 38 is divided by 4?
4 Divide 30 by 4.
5 $19 \div 4 =$ ■ remainder ▲.   6 $43 \div 4 =$ ■ remainder ▲.

63

1 How many small cubes are there in the picture? Write the number in digits.
2 Write eight hundred and eight in digits.
3 Add a half of 8 to a quarter of 12.
4 There are 4 rows of apples with 11 apples in each row. How many apples are there?
5 Write the correct sign (<, > or =) in place of ●.   26 ○ XXIV
6 Solve this equation by finding the number which can be put in place of x. $x \times 4 = 444$

64

1 Divide the total of 2, 3 and 7 by 4.
2 Find a quarter of the difference between 2 and 10.
3 Add 5 to $\frac{1}{4}$ of 20.
4 Add 4 to 5 times 4.

5 Nine oranges are cut into quarters. How many quarters are there?
6 Multiply the difference between 9 and 5 by 4.

33 thirty-three

65
1. How many are there in 8 rows of 10?
2. The product of 7 and 10 is ▨.
3. 10 × 6 = ▨.
4. How many tens are there in ninety?
5. How many tens are equal to forty?
6. 50 ÷ 10 = ▨.

66
10 times 9 = 90
10 times 8 = 80
Can you see a smart way of multiplying a number by ten?
70 ÷ 10 = 7
170 ÷ 10 = 17
Can you see a smart way of dividing a number by ten?

1. Multiply 19 by 10.
2. Find 10 times 15.
3. 10 × 20 = ▨
4. 90 ÷ 10 = ▨
5. 110 ÷ 10 = ▨
6. 210 ÷ 10 = ▨

67

1. There are 17 packets of crayons. How many crayons are there altogether?
2. How many eggs are there in ten full boxes if there are a dozen in each box?
3. There are enough marbles in a jar to give 11 boys 10 marbles each. How many marbles are in the jar?
4. How long will it take to cycle 40 kilometres at a speed of 10 kilometres an hour?
5. Mira had enough cherries to give 10 to each of her friends. If she had 70 cherries how many friends had she?
6. Ali had 67 stamps. He arranged 10 stamps in each row of his album. How many full rows had he and how many were left over?

34 thirty-four

68

1. 499 + 1 = ■.
2. The sum of three numbers is 10. The first number is 4 and the second number 5. What is the third?
3. What does 12 become when it is doubled?
4. What is the product of the odd numbers greater than 2 and less than 6?
5. How many books have Paul and Sue read altogether?
6. There are 60 books in the class library. How many has Sue still to read?

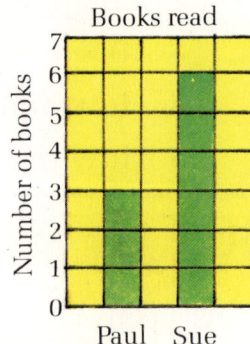

69

1. Nine fives = ■.
2. One-fifth of a number is 2. What is the number?
3. Multiply 7 by 5.
4. How many are there altogether in 8 rows if there are 5 in a row?
5. How many fives are there in twenty-five?
6. What is one-fifth of thirty?

70

1. Divide 50 by 5.
2. What is $\frac{1}{5}$ of 40?
3. How many fives are there in four tens?
4. How many tens are there in four fives?
5. What is the remainder when 38 is divided by 5?
6. If 5 children share 35 dominoes equally, how many dominoes will each child get?

71

1. How many are left over when these conkers are shared equally among 5 children?
2. 17 ÷ 5 = ■, remainder ▲.
3. 44 ÷ 5 = ■, remainder ▲.
4. Find one-fifth of the sum of nine and six.
5. Add 5 to $\frac{1}{5}$ of 10.
6. Take the product of 5 and 4 from 20.

35 thirty-five

72
1. A pack of Brownies made themselves into five rings with eight in each ring. How many Brownies were there?
2. A box held enough dates to give Sue, Lisa and Karen 5 dates each. How many dates were there?
3. Mrs Brown bought 5 boxes of Christmas cards. There were 40 cards altogether and each box held the same number. How many were in each box?
4. Claire needed 100 buttons. There were 10 buttons on a card. How many cards did she need?
5. Jane collected 5 times as many shells as Paul. Paul had 7 shells. How many shells had Jane?
6. A Christmas tree was decorated with 5 red lights, 5 blue lights, 5 yellow lights, 5 green lights and 5 white lights. How many lights were on the tree?

73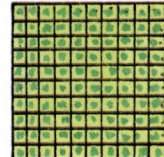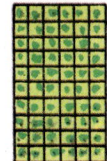

1. How many stamps are there? Write the number in digits.
2. From the sum of 3 and 5 take their difference.
3. Susan had a string of 20 beads. A fifth of the beads were blue and the rest were white. How many white beads were there?
4. Solve this equation by finding the number which can be put in place of $\boxed{r}$.
   $$17 - 8 = 4 + \boxed{r}$$
5. Solve this equation.
   $$200 - 11 = \boxed{r}$$
6. Round off the distance on the signpost to the nearest 100 kilometres.

74
1. Five threes = ■.
2. Multiply 9 by 3.
3. One-third of a number is 4. What is the number?
4. What is the product of three and eight?
5. $3 \times 10 = $ ■.
6. $3 \times 0 = $ ■ and $0 \times 3 = $ ■.

36 thirty-six

75

1. How many threes are there in twenty-one?
2. 18 ÷ 3 ▪
3. What is one-third of 27?
4. What is the remainder when 26 is divided by 3?
5. Look at the picture. How many of these apples are left over when they are shared equally among three boys?
6. $\frac{1}{3}$ of 6 + $\frac{1}{3}$ of 9 = ▪

76

1. Divide the difference between 4 and 10 by 3.
2. What is $\frac{1}{3}$ of the total of 2, 2 and 5?
3. Multiply the sum of 2 and 3 by 3.
4. How many threes are there in the sum of eight and four?
5. Write the correct sign (<, > or =) in place of ●.
   4 × 3 ● 4 × 1 × 3 × 1
6. Solve this equation. $\boxed{n}$ × 3 = 60

77

1. Here are Peter's model cars. David has three times as many. How many cars has David?

2. A girl spent 12p on balloons costing 3p each. How many did she buy?
3. Jane, Susan and Sarah each had six foreign coins. How many coins did they have altogether?
4. I am thinking of a number. 10 times that number is 30. What is the number?

5. The marbles in the picture were divided equally among Ali and his two brothers. How many marbles did each have?
6. There are 50 envelopes in a packet. How many envelopes are there altogether in 3 packets?

37 thirty-seven

78

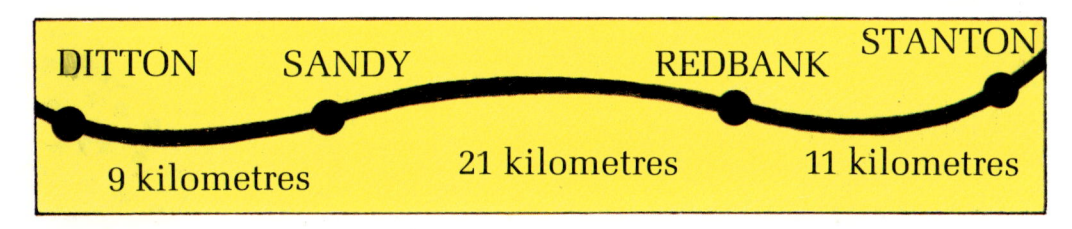

DITTON — SANDY — REDBANK — STANTON
9 kilometres — 21 kilometres — 11 kilometres

1. What is the sum of 99 and 47?
2. 143 = 120 + ▢ + 13
3. Divide the product of 6 and 2 by 4.
4. A boy had 33 picture stickers which he put into 3 equal groups. How many were there in each group?
5. The sum of two numbers is 10. Their difference is 2. What are the numbers?
6. How many kilometres is it from Ditton to Stanton?

79
1. What are five sixes?
2. Multiply 7 by 6.
3. 6 times 3 = ▢.
4. A quarter of a number is six. What is the number?
5. How many sixes are there in sixty?
6. What is $\frac{1}{6}$ of 42?

80
1. How many sixes are there in forty-eight?
2. Divide 54 by 6.
3. Six times a number is thirty-six. What is the number?
4. 24 ÷ 6 = ▢.
5. What is the remainder when 49 is divided by 6?
6. How many of these foreign stamps are left over when they are shared equally among six children?

81
1. How many sixes are equal to eight threes?
2. Divide the sum of 9 and 9 by 6.
3. What is $\frac{1}{6}$ of the sum of 7 and 5?
4. Multiply the difference between 8 and 3 by 6.
5. Add the sum of 1 and 6 to the product of 1 and 6.
6. Divide the total of 7, 4 and 1 by 6.

38 thirty-eight

82

1. There are the same number of dots on each card. How many dots are there altogether?
2. How many skittles are there in a set if there are sixty skittles in six sets?
3. Tom pasted his set of picture cards of footballers into his album. He put six cards on each of the eight pages. How many cards were in the set?
4. Two bundles of pencils were given to each of six classes. How many pencils was this altogether? 
5. Solve this equation.
    $8 \times 3 = \boxed{n} \times 6$
6. What number can you write instead of ■?
    $\blacksquare \times 6 = 606$

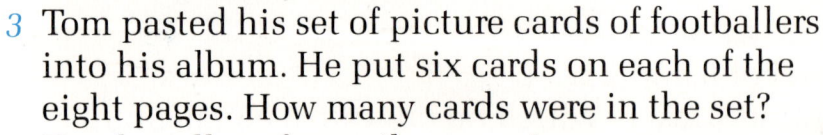

83

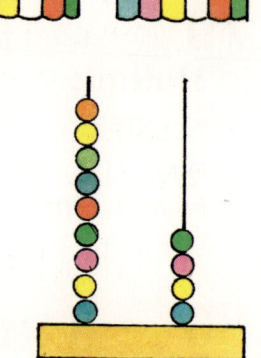

1. Write the abacus number in words.
2. Solve this equation by finding the number you can write instead of $\boxed{x}$ in this equation.
    $66 + 8 + \boxed{x} = 76$
3. Write this Roman numeral in words. **XXIV**
4. Baby Sue weighs 10 kilograms. She weighed $3\frac{1}{2}$ kilograms at birth. How many kilograms has she gained?
5. What fraction (part) of this set of stars is white? 
6. Write the missing numbers.
    497 498 ■ ■ 501

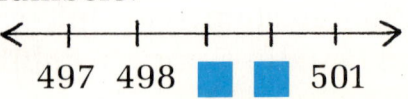

84

= means **is equal to**.
≠ means **is not equal to**.

Write = or ≠ in place of ●.

1. $7 + 9$ ● $10 + 6$
2. $18 \div 6$ ● $12 - 3$
3. $8 + 7$ ● 3×6
4. 4×6 ● 3×8
5. $17 - 6$ ● $10 + 1$
6. 6×1 ● $6 \times 0 + 1$

39 thirty-nine

85
1. I used a drinking straw to make each side of this star. How many straws would I need to make 10 stars?
2. I am thinking of a number. One-third of the number is a half of twelve. What is the number?
3. Subtract 103 from 463.
4. Write the correct sign (=, −, × or ÷) in place of ● in this equation.   9 + 9 < 12 ● 6
5. What is the sum of 123 and 110?
6. Write the correct sign (<, >, or =) in place of ●.
   XXXVI ● XXXIV

86
1. What is the difference between 120 and 99?
2. There are 23 girls and 14 boys in a recorder group. How many children are there altogether?
3. Solve this equation.   18 + v = 30
4. What number can we write in place of ■?
   30 + 40 + 60 = 30 + 60 + ■
5. For 160 we can write 1 hundred and 6 tens or ■ tens.
6. In our school hall there are 12 vases each holding the same number of flowers. How many flowers are there?

87
1. The lowest number I can build with the digits 7, 3 and 9 is 379. What is the greatest number I can build with these digits?
2. Divide the difference between 5 and 20 by 5.
3. Solve this equation.   900 + s = 909
4. Sam has 9 model cars. If he had 1 more he would have half as many as Mohammed. How many has Mohammed?
5. Fifteen children were asked if they liked chocolate or strawberry ice-cream.
   a How many like chocolate? b How many like strawberry?
6. 5 × 9 × 2 × 1 = ■

Favourite ice-cream

Money

88
1. 400 + 100 + 10 = ☐
2. Look at the pattern of the numbers below. Now write the next three numbers.
   80, 85, 90, 95, ☐, ☐, ☐ 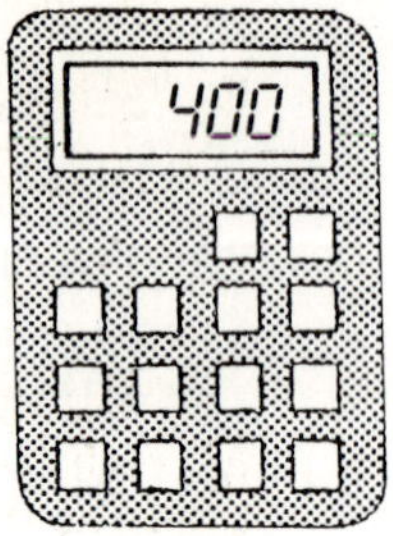
3. Write the correct sign (+, −, × or ÷) in place of ▲.
   6 ▲ 4 = 30 − 6
4. With the digits 4, 9 and 7 we can build these numbers:
   |497| |947| |974| |794| |749| |479|
   Now write down all the odd numbers you can build with the digits 7, 6 and 5.
5. How many more than the sum of 16 + 70 + 40 is the sum of 16 + 100 + 40?
6. If you multiply any number by me, the answer is 0. Who am I?

89

penny — 1p
five — 5p
ten — 10p

Count the money.

1 
2  
3 
4  
5 
6

40 forty

41 forty-one

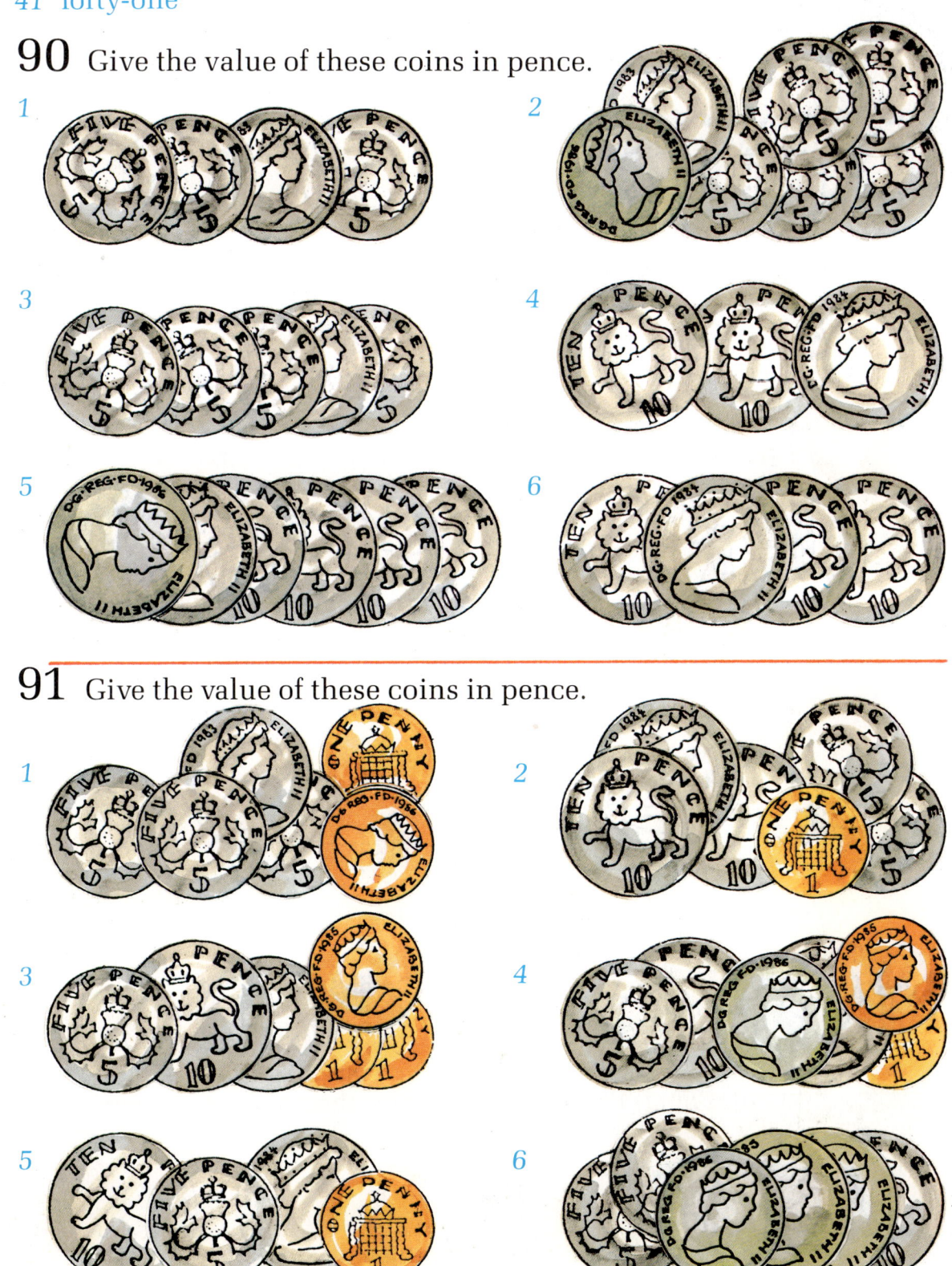

90 Give the value of these coins in pence.

1.   2.

3.   4.

5.   6.

91 Give the value of these coins in pence.

1.   2.

3.   4.

5.   6.

42 forty-two

92 How many fives are equal in value to each of these?

1

2 30 pennies   3 1 ten and 10 pennies

How many tens are equal in value to each of these?

4

5 60 pennies   6 8 fives

93 **Class 1 birthdays**

This graph shows the number of pupils in Class 1 who have birthdays in each month.

1 How many pupils are there in Class 1?
2 What is the next even number greater than 398?
3 Find the total of all the numbers greater than 4 and less than 8.
4 Take $\frac{1}{4}$ of 8 from $\frac{1}{4}$ of 20.
5 $100 + 8 + 90 = 200 - \blacksquare$.
6 I am thinking of a number. If I add 4 to the number, the answer is equal to the sum of 5 and 7. What is the number?

43 forty-three

94 Here is a two pence coin called a **two**.
Find the value in pence of each of these three
rows by counting in twos, like this: 2, 4, 6 . . .

1

2

3

Here is a twenty pence coin called a **twenty**.
Find the value in pence of each of these three
rows by counting in twenties, like this: 20, 40, 60 . . .

4

5

6

44 forty-four

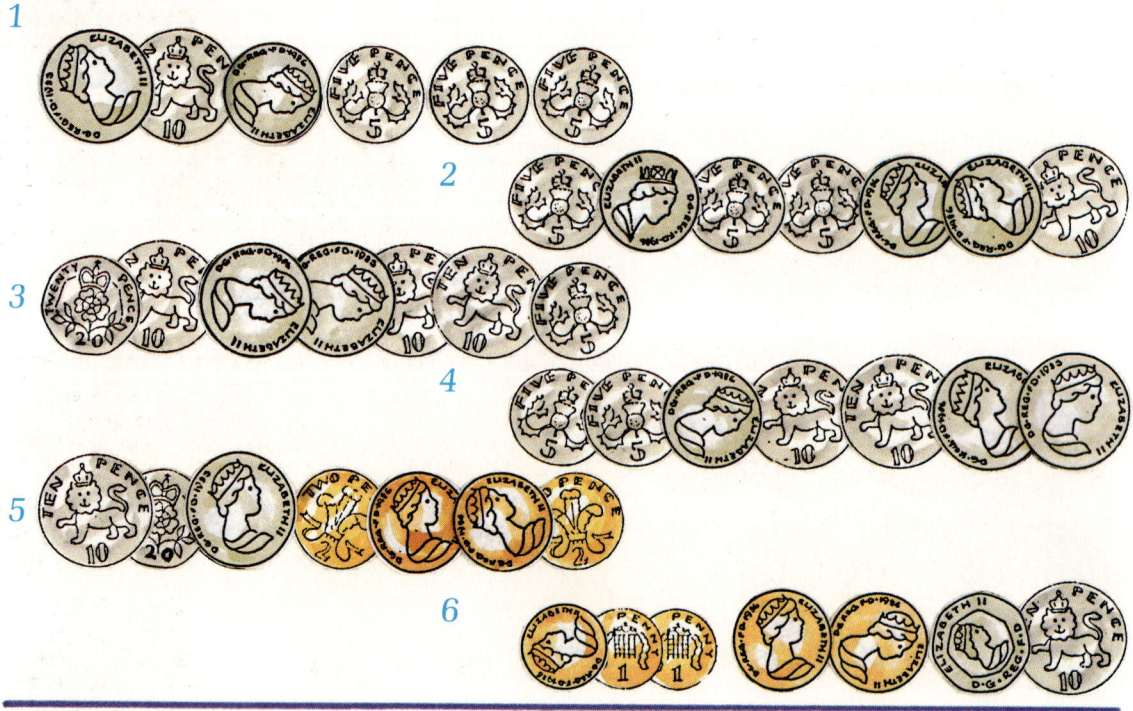

95 What is the value in pence of each of these rows of coins?

1

2

3

4

5

6

---

96 What is the value in pence of each of these rows of coins?

1

2

3

4

5

6

45 forty-five

97 What is the value of each of these in pence?

1. 2 tens and 1 five.
2. 1 ten, 1 five and 5 pennies.
3. 2 twenties, 2 twos and 2 pennies.
4. 1 ten and 10 twos.
5. 1 twenty and 10 pennies.
6. 3 fives and 5 pennies.

98

1. How many dots are there in the picture? Write the number in digits.
2. Write the correct sign (<, > or =) in place of ●.
   $$20 \div 4 \; ● \; 8 - 3$$
3. Adam has won 20 more conkers. He now has 74. How many had he before?
4. Solve this equation.
   $$50 + 20 = 100 - \boxed{n}$$
5. Remember that we can multiply numbers in any order.
   $$5 \times 7 \times 2 = \boxed{}$$
6.
   a   b   c   d

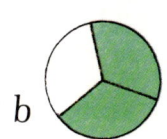

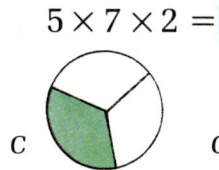

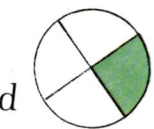

Which of these pictures is $\frac{1}{4}$ coloured?

99

1. Change 14 pennies to twos. How many are there?
2. Change 22 pennies to twos. How many are there?
3. Change 30 pennies to twos. How many are there?
4. Change 40 pennies to twenties. How many are there?
5. Change 55 pennies to fives How many are there?
6. Change 70 pennies to tens. How many are there?

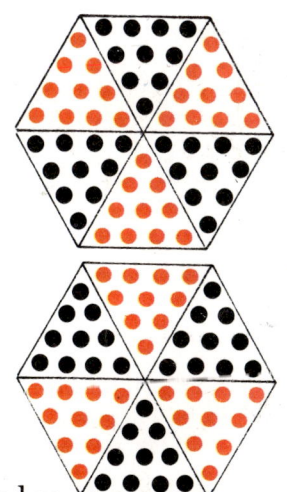

46 forty-six

100
1. What is the cost of 24 sweets at two pence each?
2. Sarah had 28p in twos. How many coins did she have?
3. How many fives are fair exchange for two 10p pieces?
4. Crayons cost 5p each. How many can you buy with 3 tens?
5. Sam gave a twenty to pay for a lemonade costing 16p. He got his change in pennies. How many pennies did he get?
6. Class 3 clubbed together to buy a Christmas gift for their teacher. Each pupil gave a two, and 68p was collected altogether. How many pupils were in the class?

101 Here is a fifty pence coin called a **fifty**.
1. How many fives can be changed for a fifty?
2. How many tens are worth two fifties?
3. How many twos are worth a fifty?
4. What is the total value of a fifty and 2 twenties?
5. How many tens are equal in value to 3 fifties?
6. How many twenties are equal in value to 2 fifties?

102

This drawing shows the number of pennies equal in value to a pound (£1).
1. How many pennies are equal in value to £2?
2. How many tens are equal in value to £1?
3. How many twenties can be given for £1?
4. How many two pence coins (twos) are equal in value to a pound?
5. How many fifties are equal in value to £3?
6. How many pence would be left from £1 after spending a twenty?

47 forty-seven

103

1 Each box in the picture holds ten coloured pencils.

How many pencils are there altogether?

2 60 + 7 = 50 + ■

3 Find the difference between 40 and 23.

4 Look at the pattern of these numbers, then write the next three numbers.

60, 56, 52, 48, ■, ■, ■.

5 David had 188 stamps in his collection.

He bought 12 more.

How many did he have then?

6 This helicopter flies at a speed of 80 kilometres an hour.

How far will it fly in a quarter of an hour?

104

1 What is the cost of the box of games and the racing car?
2 Find the cost of the racing car and the writing set.
3 How much is the box of paints and the game?
4 What is the cost of the paints and the writing set?
5 A boy paid for the box of paints with a ten, two fives and some twos. How many twos did he use?
6 A girl paid for the writing set with a fifty, a five and a number of pennies. How many pennies were there?

48 forty-eight

105
1. 4p + 16p = ☐p
2. 79p + 11p = ☐p
3. 17p + 5p = ☐p
4. 18p + 12p = ☐p
5. 16p + 12p = ☐p
6. 27p + 33p = ☐p

106 Carol's money

1. What is the total of 17p, 15p and 3p?
2. How much is 16p and 8p?
3. Add together 8p, 16p and 4p.
4. A boy got 33p change after spending 17p. What coin had he given the shopkeeper?
5. Jane has 15p, Fiona 4p and Sabina 5p. How much do they have altogether?
6. In Carol's purse there are 4 fives, 4 pennies and 4 twos. How much money has she altogether?

107

1. Find the total of 40p, 10p and 30p.
2. Sue had 12p left after losing a five and spending 7p. How much had she at first?
3. Work out the total cost of a ruler costing 30p and 2 packets of envelopes costing 30p each.
4. How much does Adam need to buy a ball pen for 60p and two refills costing 20p each?
5. A girl had 17p and was given a twenty. How much did she have then?
6. Ali spent 12p on potato crisps, 27p on a comic and had 3p left. How much did he have to start with?

49 forty-nine

108
1. Write eight hundred and eighty-one in digits.
2. A boy has 100 marbles. 45 are striped. How many other marbles are there?
3. Ten boys had to carry a total of 120 chairs into the school hall. They each carried the same number.
   How many chairs did each boy carry?
4. Divide the product of 5 and 10 by the difference between 5 and 10.
5. There are 28 pupils in Class 2. We can see from the picture that 7 of them cycle to school. How many pupils go to school by car?
6. Look at the picture again. How many pupils do not walk to school?

109
1. 10p − 4p = ☐p
2. 80p − 20p = ☐p
3. 20p − 3p = ☐p
4. 59p − 40p = ☐p
5. 17p − 4p = ☐p
6. 98p − 30p = ☐p

110
1. 30p − 8p = ☐p
2. 80p − 65p = ☐p
3. 60p − 6p = ☐p
4. 70p − 15p = ☐p
5. 52p − 4p = ☐p
6. 40p − 13p = ☐p

111
1. 55p − 15p = ☐p
2. 31p − 11p = ☐p
3. 30p − 11p = ☐p
4. 44p − 7p = ☐p
5. 25p − 16p = ☐p
6. 52p − 13p = ☐p

112 How much change would you get?
1. 5p, 2p, 2p
2. 8p, 50p
3. 7p, 5p, 5p
4. 25p, 50p
5. 11p, 10p, 10p
6. 70p, 50p, 50p

50 fifty

113

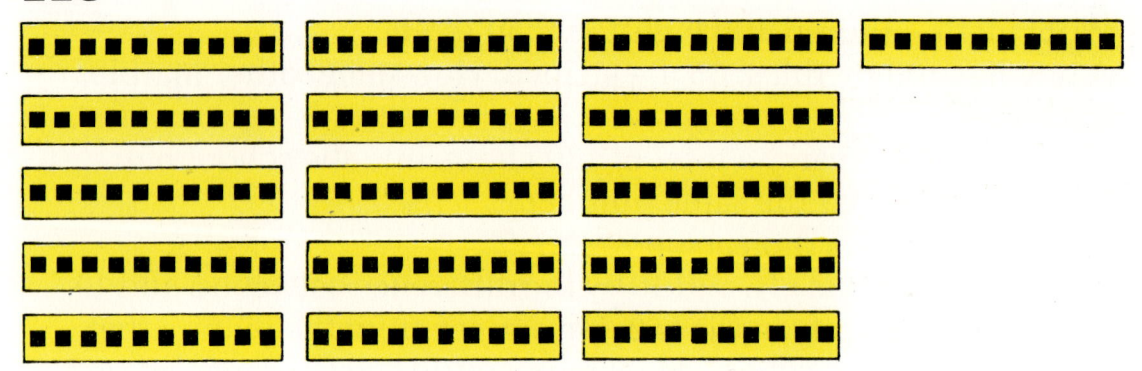

1. How many squares are there? Write the number in digits.
2. The product of two numbers is 30. One of the numbers is 6. What is the other number?
3. What number must be taken from 50 to leave 35?
4. Jeff needs 20 more picture cards for a full set.
   There are 52 cards in a set.
   How many cards has Jeff now?
5. How many tens are equal in value to 4 fives?
6. This box of chocolates has one layer.
   How many chocolates are in the box?

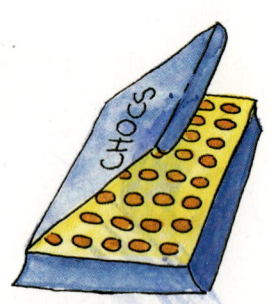

114

1. What change would you get from 2 tens if you spent 17p?
2. Shakira needed 9p to make her money up to 90p. How much did she have?
3. How much less than 20p is 9p?
4. What change is received from 2 twenties after spending 25p?
5. A bus fare was 55p. What change was received from 3 twenties?
6. How much change was received from a fifty after spending 29p?

115

1. How much was left out of a fifty after spending five pence?
2. How much is 17p short of 70p?
3. Subtract 11p from 80p.
4. How much more than 15p is 50p?
5. Make 14p up to 30p. How much do you need?
6. 'A Book of Stars' costs 95p. Jean has 7 tens.
   How much more does she need?

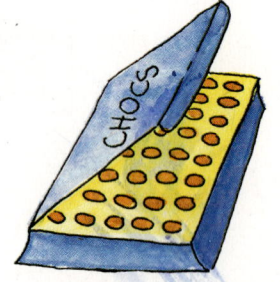

51 fifty-one

116

1 How much was left from 2 tens after spending 7p and 4p?
2 What change had I from a twenty after spending 9p and 8p?
3 Take the sum of 6p and 9p from 25p.
4 How much less than 50p is the total of 7p, 5p and 3p?
5 Jill had 3 fives. How much had she left after spending 8p?
6 A boy had 2 fifties. He bought a bicycle bell. How much did he have left?

117

1 What must you add to 30p to make £1?
2 How many twos are worth two twenties?
3 5 pennies and 5 tens = ▇p.
4 Change 60 pennies into fives. How many are there?
5 Solve this equation. $\boxed{n}$ pence + 12 pence = 90p
6 Tom has 15p and Peter has 15p more than Tom. How much do they have altogether?

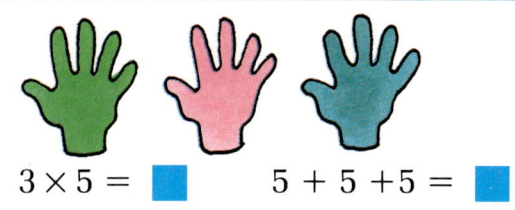

118

$3 \times 5 =$ ▇ $5 + 5 + 5 =$ ▇

1 Write the two number sentences above in full.
2 7 cars, 5 coaches and 3 lorries are in a car park. How many vehicles are there?
3 160 = 10 + ▇ + 100
4 How many tens are equal in value to 5 twenties?
5 Which three coins would you use to make 53p?
6 Last season a school team scored 33 goals. 14 of these were scored by the captain. How many other goals were scored?

52 fifty-two

119
1. 6 gobstoppers cost ☐ p.
2. 3 chews cost ☐ p.
3. 2 sugar mice cost ☐ p.
4. 5 chocolate fingers cost ☐ p.
5. 4 ice-creams cost ☐ p.
6. 10 candy sticks cost ☐ p.

120
1. 2 mini lollies cost ☐ p.
2. 2 small cones cost ☐ p.
3. 2 large cones cost ☐ p.
4. 2 tubs cost ☐ p.
5. 2 sundaes cost ☐ p.
6. 2 choc ices cost ☐ p.

121
1. 2 bananas cost ☐ p.
2. 2 lemons cost ☐ p.
3. 10 apples cost ☐ p.
4. 5 pears cost ☐ p.
5. 4 oranges cost ☐ p.
6. 3 cucumbers cost ☐ p.

53 fifty-three

122

1. 2 pens cost ▧ p.
2. 4 sharpeners cost ▧ p.
3. 6 notebooks cost ▧ p.
4. 4 rulers cost ▧ p.
5. 6 pencils cost ▧ p.
6. 5 rubbers cost ▧ p.

123

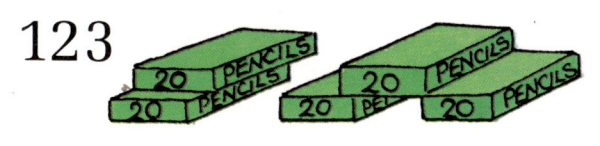

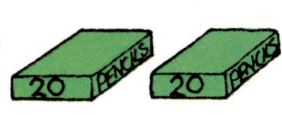

1. How many pencils are there in this picture? Write the number in digits.
2. Take a third of 18 from a half of 18.
3. What is the remainder when 50 is divided by 4?
4. Write the correct sign (>, < or =) in place of ●.
   8 ÷ 4 ● 4 × 2
5. How many twos are equal in value to 4 fives?
6. A boy has four twenties. How much more does he need to buy the dartboard in the picture?

124

4 peaches cost 80p. What is the cost of 1 peach?
Think: 80 ÷ 4 = 20
1 peach costs 20p.

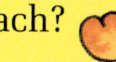

Work out these divisions.

1. 14p ÷ 2 = ▧ p
2. 21p ÷ 3 = ▧ p
3. 40p ÷ 2 = ▧ p
4. 30p ÷ 3 = ▧ p
5. 24p ÷ 2 = ▧ p
6. 80p ÷ 4 = ▧ p

125

1 30p ÷ 2 = ☐p
2 32p ÷ 4 = ☐p
3 48p ÷ 2 = ☐p
4 60p ÷ 3 = ☐p
5 70p ÷ 2 = ☐p
6 50p ÷ 5 = ☐p

126

1 45p ÷ 5 = ☐p
2 90p ÷ 3 = ☐p
3 24p ÷ 4 = ☐p
4 50p ÷ 2 = ☐p
5 36p ÷ 6 = ☐p
6 44p ÷ 4 = ☐p

127

1 What is a quarter of 28p?

2 Divide 36p by 3.

3 Find $\frac{1}{3}$ of 45p

4 Work out one-fifth of 55p

5 38p ÷ 2 = ☐p

6 What is half of 80p?

55 fifty-five

128   ④⑤⑥

1 What is the greatest number you can build using these digits?
2 Write the correct sign (>, < or =) in place of ●.
   10 − 4 ● 48 ÷ 6
3 Look at the pattern of these numbers carefully, then write the next two numbers.
   $1\frac{1}{2}$, 3, $4\frac{1}{2}$, ■, ■.
4 40p was made up of 5 fives and some pennies. How many pennies were there?
5 What is the total cost of 2 ice lollies at 25p each and 2 choc ices at 25p each?
6 Look at the picture. There are ten of these stacks of chairs. How many chairs are there altogether?

129

1 Share a five and 2 twenties equally among 5 children.
2 Abu spent 77p on buying an ice lolly each day for a week. How much were the lollies each?
3 Jenny paid 99p in bus fares for herself and two friends. How much was one fare?
4 What is the cost of $\frac{1}{4}$ kilogram of black grapes if $\frac{1}{2}$ kilogram costs 70p?
5 Four packets of pop-corn cost 80p. How much is one packet?
6 What is the value of one of the tins of dog food in the picture?

56 fifty-six

130

1. Change 38 pennies into twos.
2. How many pennies are equal in value to 7 fives?
3. How many tens are equal in value to the sum of 14p and 16p?
4. What must be added to 10 pennies to be equal in value to 3 fives?
5. How many pennies are needed to make 84p up to £1?
6. What is the cost of 10 apples?

131

1. How many chocolate shapes can I get for a ten, if they are 2 for a penny?
2. At the fair, Peter spent 45p on the Dodgems and 55p on pony rides. How much did he spend?
3. Three boys and three girls each gave 9p to buy a friend a present. How much did the present cost?
4. John sold 4 tickets for a school concert. If he had £1 ticket money, what was the cost of a ticket?
5. Lisa bought a ruler for 48p and a pencil for 12p. How much had she to pay?
6. What is the total value of these stamps?

132

1. How many twos are equal in value to 2 twenties?
2. If I had another 11p, I would have £1. How much do I have?
3. 19p + 17p + 1p = ▢p
4. What is the cost of half a pineapple? 
5. Work out the cost of 4 grapefruit at 22p each.
6. I paid 3 tens for 5 boxes of matches. What was the price of one box?

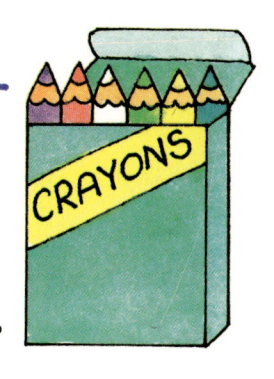

133

1. How many crayons are there in twenty boxes?
2. Find a quarter of the product of 8 and 3.
3. Half Jane's money is 49p. How much does she have?
4. Write the number 19 in Roman numerals.
5. Write out this subtraction in full.
   1 6 0
   − ▢▢
     9 0
6. I am thinking of an amount of money. If I add 7p to the amount, it would be equal in value to 4 fives. What is the amount of money?

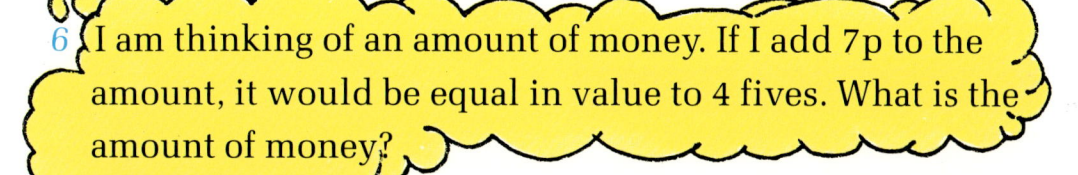

Length

58 fifty-eight

134 Here is a ruler divided into 10 equal parts.

Each small part is called a **centimetre** (1 cm).

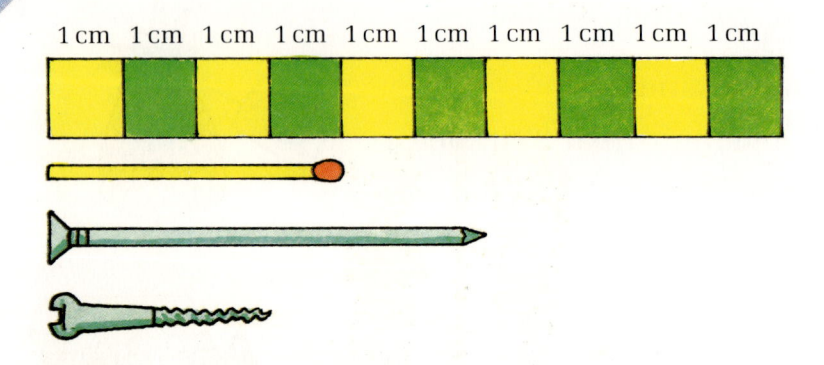

1 cm 1 cm 1 cm 1 cm 1 cm 1 cm 1 cm 1 cm 1 cm 1 cm

1 What is the length of the match?
2 What is the length of the nail?
3 What is the length of the screw?

Here is another ruler marked off in centimetres and half centimetres.

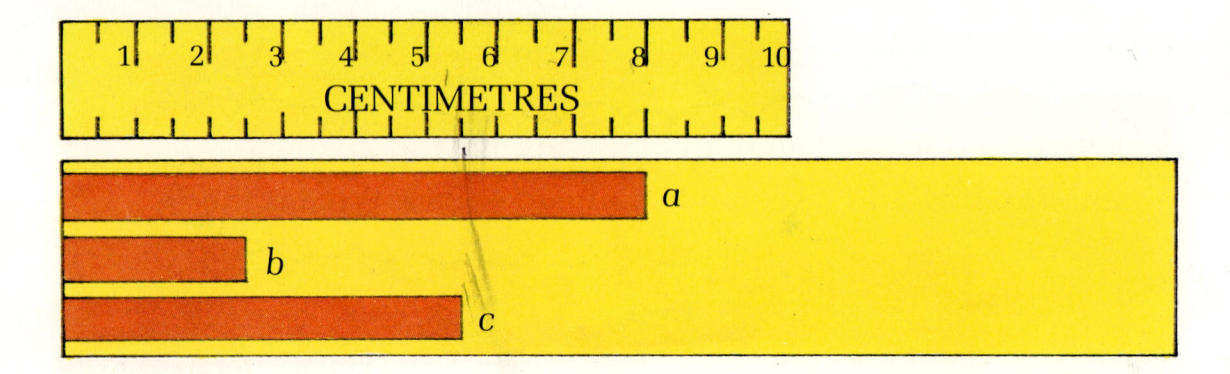

CENTIMETRES

4 How long is bar *c*?
5 How much longer is bar *a* than bar *c*?
6 How much longer is bar *a* than bar *b*?

59 fifty-nine

135

100 centimetres = 1 metre (1 m)

1 m = 100 cm

Write these in centimetres.
1. 1 metre and 65 centimetres
2. 8 metres
3. 1 m and 70 cm
4. 9 m and 9 cm
5. 6 m and 55 cm
6. 5 m and 15 cm

136

1000 metres = 1 kilometre (1 km)

1 km = 1000 m   5 km = 5000 m

1. How many metres are there in 9 km and 700 m?
2. How many metres are there in 6 km and 100 m?
3. How many metres are there in 4 km and 50 m?
4. Change 1700 m to kilometres and metres.
5. Change 3500 m to km and m.
6. Change 2020 m to km and m.

137 How many metres are needed to make these up to a kilometre?

1 400 metres
2 950 metres
3 900 metres
4 250 metres
5 990 metres
6 840 metres

138

1 How many centimetres are there in 2 metres?
2 How many metres are there in $1\frac{1}{2}$ kilometres?
3 How many metres are there in $\frac{1}{4}$ kilometre?
4 Write 250 centimetres in metres and centimetres.
5 How many metres are there in 1 kilometre and 20 metres?
6 How many centimetre rods placed end to end would measure half a metre?

139

1 How many centimetres are there in ten metres?
2 How many centimetres are there in 11 m?
3 How many 10 cm lengths are there in a metre?
4 How many centimetres are there in 12 m and 50 cm?
5 How many centimetres are there in 15 m and 25 cm?
6 How many centimetres are there in 16 m and 6 cm?

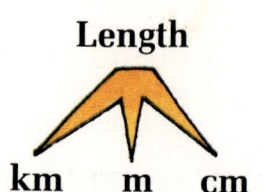

61 sixty-one

140 Write the answers only.

1 60 cm + 90 cm = ☐ m and △ cm
2 3 m and 20 cm + 90 cm = ☐ m and △ cm
3 1 m and 90 cm + 80 cm = ☐ m and △ cm
4 2 m and 70 cm + 1 m and 70 cm = ☐ m and △ cm
5 Susan has grown 40 cm in 6 years. She is now 1 m 39 cm tall. How tall was she six years ago?
6 Ann's doll is 58 cm tall. Ann is 52 cm taller. How tall is Ann in m and cm?

141

1 The tallest boy in a class is $1\frac{1}{2}$ m in height. The tallest girl is 15 cm shorter. How tall is the girl in centimetres?
2 From 2 m 10 cm take 20 cm.
3 Subtract 1 m 40 cm from 2 m.
4 Take 1 m 90 cm from 2 m 20 cm.
5 3 m − 30 cm = ☐ and △ cm
6 A roll holds $\frac{1}{2}$ metre of tape. If 10 cm are used, how much remains?

Mass (Weight)

62 sixty-two

142

1 Find the total of 900, 6 and 6000.

2 What number can be put in place of ■ in this equation?

$(6 \times 9) + 6 = $ ■ $- 6$

3 Solve this equation. $75 + 69 + n = 169$

4 Look how these numbers grow. Write the next two numbers.

0, 40, 80, 120, 160, ?, ?

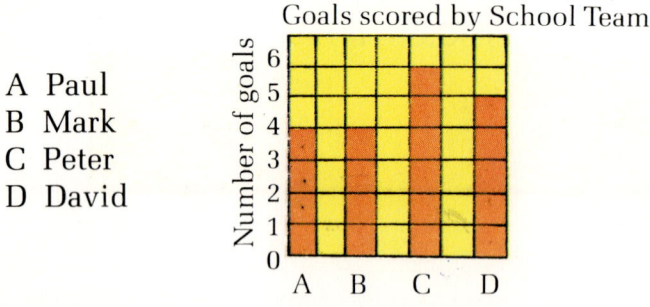

A Paul
B Mark
C Peter
D David

Goals scored by School Team

5 Look at the graph. How many goals were scored altogether?

6 How much change would be received from a £5 note after spending 40p and 60p?

143 Here is the set of objects in my pocket.

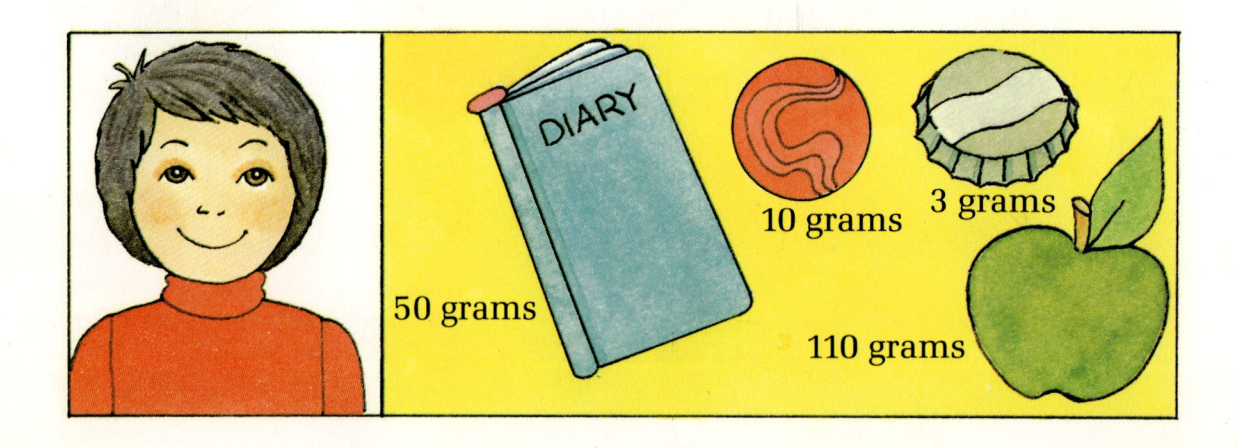

50 grams

10 grams

3 grams

110 grams

63 sixty-three

1. How much heavier is the apple than the diary?
2. How much heavier is the apple than the marble?
3. What is the total weight of all the objects?
4. How much heavier is the apple than all the other things together?
5. How many marbles would be equal in weight to the apple?
6. How many bottle tops are equal in weight to the marble and diary?

144

1000 grams = 1 kilogram (1 kg)

1 kg = 1000 g

David's dictionary weighs **1 kilogram and 200 grams** or **1200 grams**.

1. How many grams are there in 1 kg and 700 g?
2. How many grams are there in 3 kg and 30 g?
3. Write 4400 grams in kg and g.
4. Write 6070 grams in kg and g.
5. How many grams less than a kilogram is 600 g?
6. How many grams less than a kilogram is 940 g?

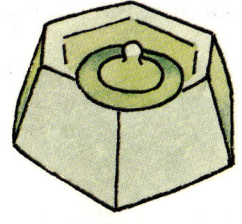

1 kilogram

64 sixty-four

145

1. How many grams are there in $1\frac{1}{2}$ kilograms?
2. A packet of tea weighs 125 g. How many packets weigh $\frac{1}{2}$ kilogram?
3. How many bars of chocolate each weighing 100 g would weigh 1 kilogram?
4. How many packets of butter each weighing 250 g would have a total weight of 1 kilogram?

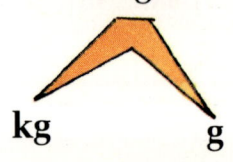

5. Arrange these weights in order of size, starting with the smallest.

   | $1\frac{1}{2}$ kg | 500 g | 1750 g | 1 kg and 90 g |

6. Three chocolate biscuits together weigh 100 g. How many would weigh a kilogram?

146

What is the total in grams of each of these collections of weights?

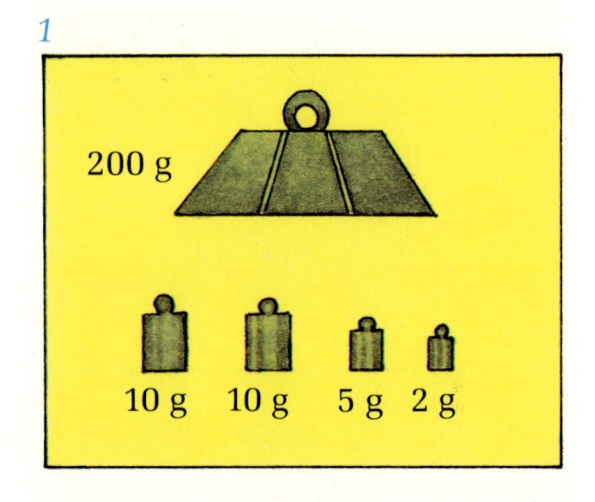

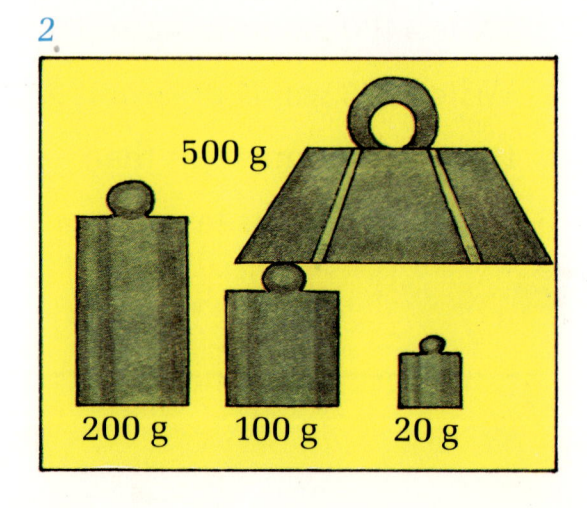

1. 200 g, 10 g, 10 g, 5 g, 2 g

2. 500 g, 200 g, 100 g, 20 g

65 sixty-five

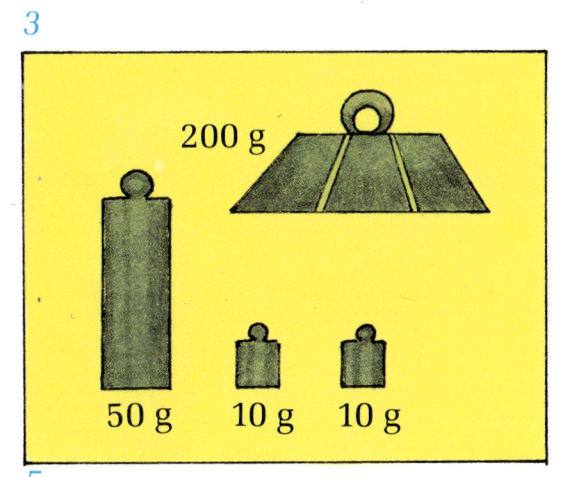

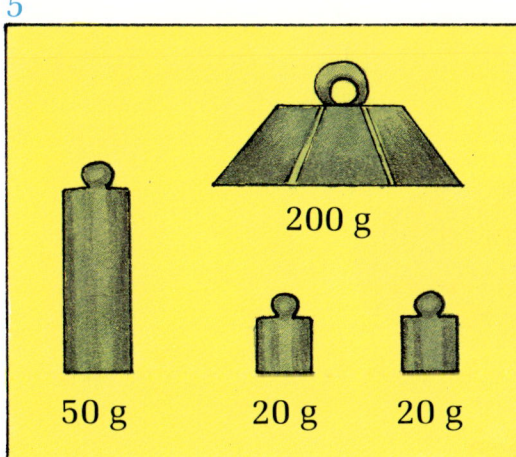

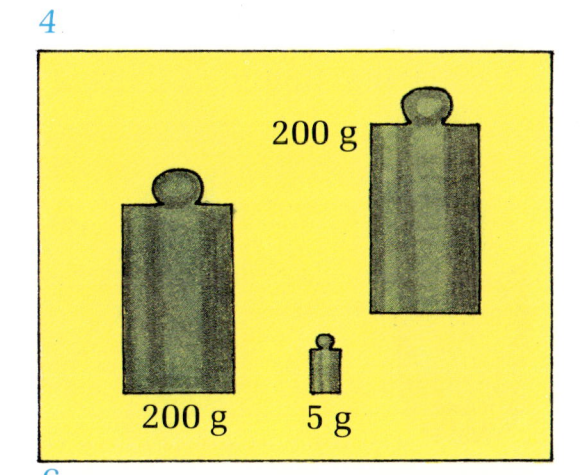

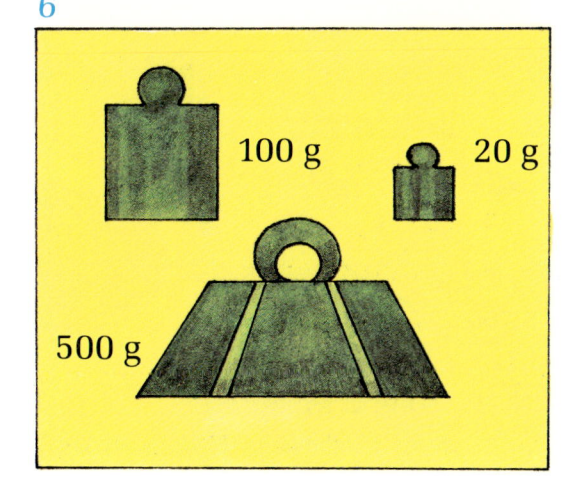

3

200 g
50 g   10 g   10 g

4

200 g
200 g   5 g

5

200 g
50 g   20 g   20 g

6

100 g   20 g
500 g

147

What are the weights of these objects? Choose the most suitable answer from the weights in brackets.

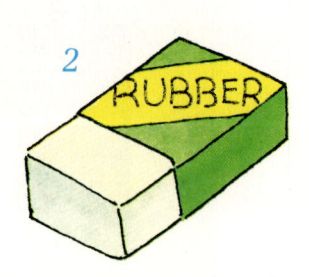

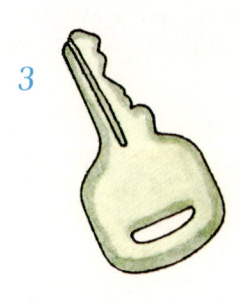

1
2
3
4

(45 g, 450 g, 4 g)   (350 g, 35 g, 3 g)   (10 g, 100 g, 1 g)   (800 g, 80 g, 8 g)

5
6

(200 g, 20 g, 2 g)   (1 g, 10 g, 100 g)

148

1000 grams = 1 kilogram (kg)

A parcel weighs **4 kg and 300 g** or **4300 g**.
Now try these.
1 How many grams are there in 1 kg and 200 g?
2 How many grams are there in 3 kg?
3 Bring 1 kg and 900 g to grams.
4 Change $1\frac{1}{2}$ kg to grams.
5 Find the number of grams in $\frac{3}{4}$ kg.
6 Bring 2 kg and 20 g to grams.

67 sixty-seven

149

1 Write in digits the number which is nine hundred and nine more than nine thousand.
2 Write out this addition in full:
$$\begin{array}{r} \blacksquare \\ +\ 602 \\ \hline 910 \end{array}$$
3 Solve this equation.
$$350 + 500 = 1000 - n$$
4 Which sign (+, −, × or ÷) should be placed instead of ■ in this equation?
$$420 + 180 = 550\ \blacksquare\ 50$$
5 What is the total cost of 5 slices of custard tart and 5 glasses of milk?
6 How many centimetres are there in $4\frac{1}{2}$ metres?

150

1 How many kilograms are there in 9000 grams?
2 Bring 3070 g to kg and g.
3 Change 4250 g to kilograms.
4 How many kg and g are there in 2007 g?
5 Bring 3600 g to kg and g.
6 How many $\frac{1}{2}$ kg are there in 1500 grams?

Capacity

68 sixty-eight

151

1. How many litres of orange juice are needed to give 36 pupils a quarter of a litre each?
2. A family takes $1\frac{1}{2}$ litres of milk a day. How many litres is this a week?
3. An oil tank holds 118 litres of oil. How many litres are left when 20 litres are taken out?
4. How many $\frac{1}{4}$-litre glasses can be filled from 4 litres of lemonade?
5. We know that a litre of water weighs 1 kilogram. What is the weight of $1\frac{1}{2}$ litres of water in grams?
6. A car travels 100 kilometres on 8 litres of petrol. How many litres of petrol would be needed for a journey of 400 kilometres?

152

151   157   88   59

1. Add the greatest and the least of the calculator numbers.
2. What number is 8 less than the sum of 7 and 5?
3. One-quarter of a number is 9. What is half of the number?
4. Ann has two tens and 11 pennies. How much more does she need to buy a sharpener costing 40p?
5. Arrange these lengths in order of size starting with the smallest.

    | 1 km | 100 cm | 1100 m | $\frac{1}{2}$ km |

6. A bag of potatoes weighs 3 kilograms. How many grams is this?

69 sixty-nine

153

Checking Up

1 Write in digits the number which is 1 less than a thousand.

2 Find the sum of twice 6 and three times 6.

3 Write out this addition in full:
$$\begin{array}{r} 3 \\ + \ 4\ 6 \\ \hline 7 \end{array}$$

4 There are 4 slices in a quarter of a cut loaf. How many slices are there in a whole loaf?

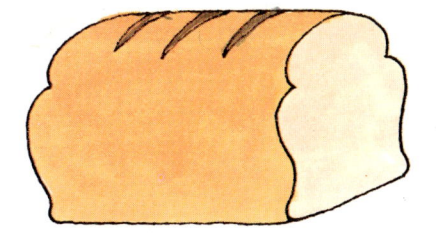

5 Orange cream biscuits are 3 for 10p. How many can be bought with a fifty?

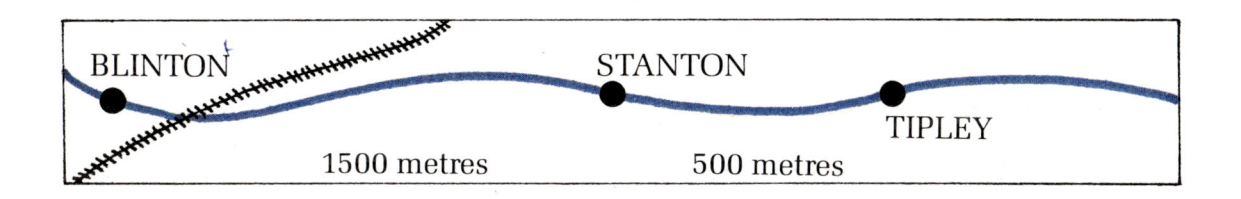

BLINTON   STANTON
                              TIPLEY
     1500 metres   500 metres

6 What is the distance from Blinton to Tipley in kilometres?

70 seventy

154

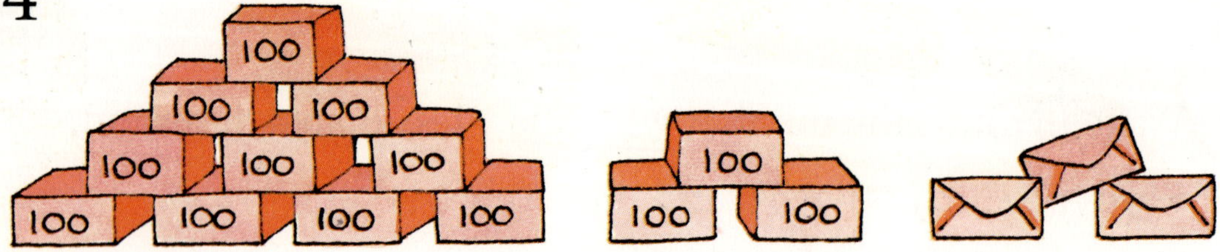

1. How many envelopes are there? Write the numeral in digits.
2. What number can we put in place of ■?

    $4 + 9 + 7 = 9 + $ ■ $ + 7$

3. How many less than 10 is the sum of the odd numbers between 2 and 6?
4. Sam spent 15p and 25p. He was then given a ten change. What coin had he handed the shopkeeper?
5. What is the cost of $1\frac{1}{2}$ kg of puppy meal at 50p a kilogram?
6. What is the total weight in kilograms of ten 500 gram packs of butter?

155

1. Write in digits two thousand and twenty.
2. How many sixes are equal to the product of 9 and 4?
3. Write out this addition in full:

    ▲ 3
      1 9
    + 5 2
    ─────
    1 0 ■

71 seventy-one

4 How many crayons at 3 for 7p can I buy for 35p?

5 A gardener put 250 grams of seeds into packets.

He put 10 grams in each packet.

How many packets were there?

6 Rani is 1 metre and 14 centimetres tall.

What is her height in centimetres?

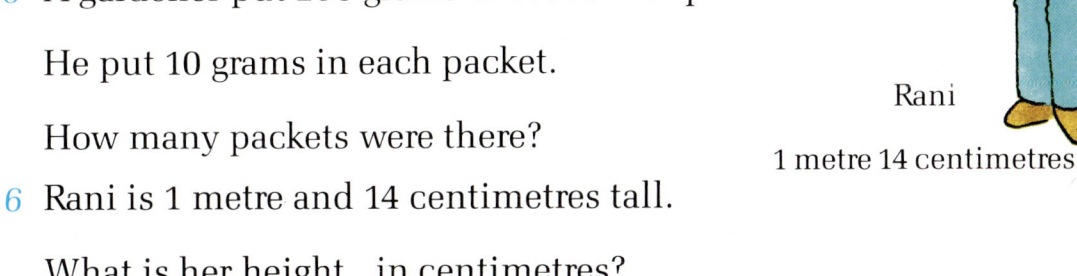

Rani
1 metre 14 centimetres

156

1 Write in digits the number shown above.

2 Multiply the difference between 9 and 4 by 5.

3 Write the correct sign (>, < or =) in place of ●.

$$67 + 10 \quad ● \quad 97 - 10$$

4 Jaswant had 140 cm of wire. He cut off 50 cm. How much was left?

5 How many grams less than half a kilogram are 400 grams?

6 Roger has 50p and Emma 20p. If they shared their money equally, how much would each have?

157

1. Write the numeral shown on the calculator in words.
2. The sum of two numbers is 1000. One of the numbers is 950. What is the other?
3. Write the correct sign (>, < or =) in place of ●.

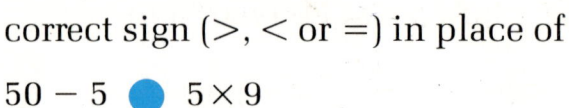

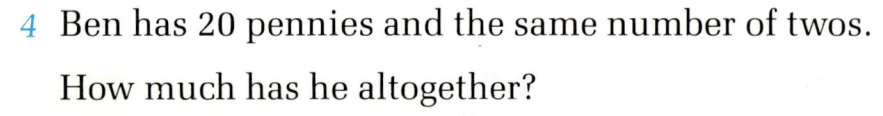

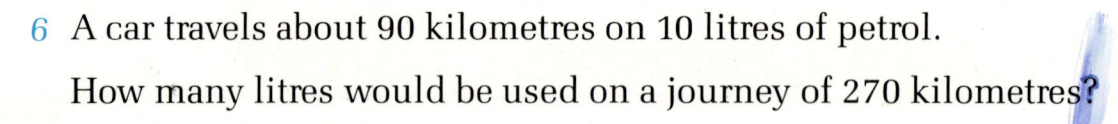

    50 − 5 ● 5 × 9

4. Ben has 20 pennies and the same number of twos. How much has he altogether?
5. 1 km − 300 m = ▣ m
6. A car travels about 90 kilometres on 10 litres of petrol. How many litres would be used on a journey of 270 kilometres?

158

1. Write in digits the next even number greater than three hundred and eighty-eight.
2. What is half the difference between 6 and 20?
3. Find the sum of 11, 10 and 9.
4. How much change would you have from £1 if you had to pay 65p?
5. David cycled 100 kilometres in 5 hours. If he kept up the same speed, how far did he cycle in one hour?
6. A shopkeeper weighed out a kilogram of sweets into 100-gram packets. How many packets were there?

73 seventy-three
159

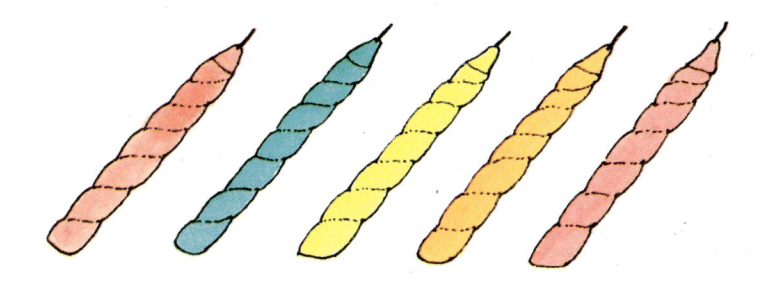

1 Write the numeral one thousand and seventeen in digits.

2 I am thinking of a number. If I add 9 and then 7, the answer is 20. What is the number?

3 In one bag there are 8 conkers and in another 7. If they are shared equally among 3 boys, how many will each have?

4 What is the cost of 20 birthday cake candles at 5 for 6p?

5 Sandra is 75 cm tall. Jamila is twice as tall. How tall is Jamila in centimetres?

6 Two kilograms of coffee are made up into 4 equal packets. What is the weight of each packet in grams?

74 seventy-four

160

1 Each box holds 100 drinking straws. How many drinking straws are there ? Write the numeral in words.
2 Solve this equation: 9 + 8 = $\boxed{n}$ + 7. 
3 Find the sum of 80, 30 and 20.
4 When I cut some apples into quarters, there were 40 pieces.
How many apples had I cut?
5 What change would I get from a fifty after buying 2 peaches at 15p each?
6 Peter's table is $1\frac{1}{2}$ metres long. How many 10-centimetre rods can he place end to end across the table?

161

1 Write the number below in Roman numerals.

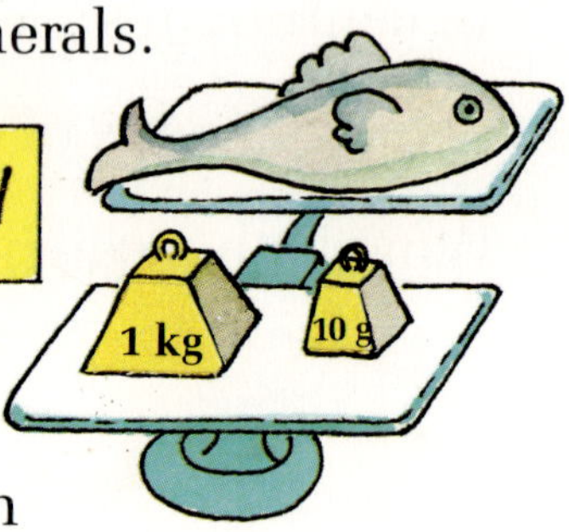

|///////// | ///////// | ///////// | ///

2 Find the number we can put in place of ■.
    16 + 4 + ■ = 25 + 5
3 Karen had 2 photographs left after putting 6 on each of the 3 pages of her new album.
How many photographs did she have altogether?
4 How many sixes are there in the sum of 9 and 9?
5 2 m − 20 cm = ■ cm
6 What is the weight of this fish in grams?

75 seventy-five

162

1 Write the number four thousand and forty in digits.
2 17 + 19 + 1 = ▨
3 Divide the sum of 6 and 4 by the difference between 6 and 4.
4 A boy had 25 picture cards. How many had he left after giving 11 to each of his two friends?
5 A packet of dates weighs 250 grams. How many packets weigh a kilogram?
6 This picture shows part of a thermometer. The temperature shown is 42°C. The temperature fell 12° and then rose 8°. The temperature was then ▨ °C.

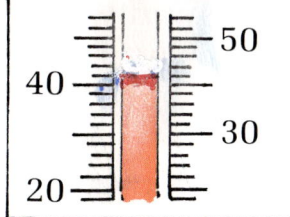

163

1 Add 101 to the number shown on this calculator.   **99**
2 What is the product of the odd numbers which are greater than 2 and less than 6?
3 Look at the bar chart. How many members are there altogether in the Friendly Club?

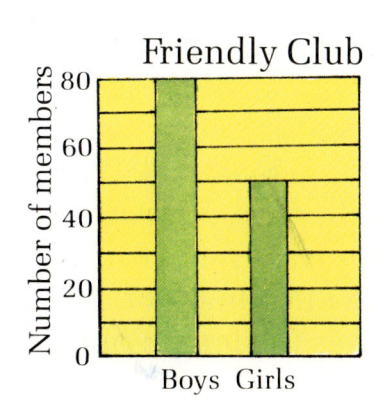

Friendly Club

76 seventy-six

4 A pet shop had a hundred goldfish. 7 were sold on Friday and 20 on Saturday. How many were left?
5 Carol has 2 twenties and twice as many tens. How many pence has she?
6 Abdul's apple weighs 100 g. How many apples of the same weight would there be in $1\frac{1}{2}$ kg?

164

1 What is a half of nine hundred? Write the answer in words.
2 A quarter of the difference between two numbers is 10. The greater number is 90. What is the smaller number?
3 Peter paid for this mask with one twenty and the rest in fives. How many fives did he use?
4 Usha cut an orange into two equal parts. She then cut each of these parts in half. What fraction of the whole was each piece?
5 How much did it cost to post this letter?
6 1 km − ▇ m = 750 m

165

1 How many small cubes are shown in this picture? Write the numeral in digits.
2 Who are we? If you add us, you get 14. If you subtract us, you get 4.
3 There are 40 members of the Dolphin Swimming Club.
  a How many learners are there?
  b How many life-savers are there?
4 I have a fifty, a twenty and a ten. How much more do I need to make £1?
5 Mr Tibbs jogged every day except Sundays for six weeks. How many days did he jog?
6 A 1-metre length of tape is cut into 20 equal pieces. What is the length of each piece?

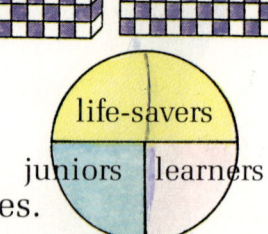

Dolphin Club

77 seventy-seven

166

1. Write the numerals between: 998, ■, ■, ■, 1002.
2. Divide 28 by 4; add 3; multiply by 10; subtract 2.
3. A class made 10 of these cotton reel models.
   How many reels were used?
4. Toffee chews are 3 for 5p.
   How many can I buy with 3 tens?
5. Jenny is exactly 1 metre in height. When her height was last measured it was $89\frac{1}{2}$ cm.
   How many centimetres has Jenny grown?
6. How many grams more than $\frac{1}{2}$ kg are 1050 grams?

167

1. How many rods are shown in this picture?
   Write the numeral in words.
2. Write this equation in full: ■ − 550 = 550.
3. What is the greatest odd number less than a thousand?
   Write the numeral in digits.
4. Each box is the same weight.
   What is the weight of one box?
5. $\frac{1}{2}$ km + 1500 m = ■ km
6. A packet of nuts weighs 200 grams.
   How many packets weigh 2 kilograms?

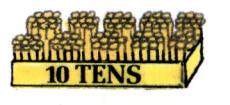

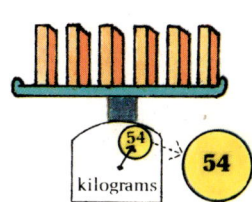

168

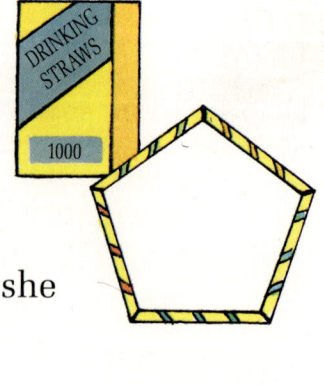

1. How many of these pentagons can be made from a full box of drinking straws?
2. 8 hundreds + 9 tens + 10 units = ◼
3. What is a quarter of the product of 3 and 8?
4. When Jane had cut some apples into quarters, she found there were 36 pieces. How many apples had been cut?
5. Write the correct sign (>, < or =) in place of each ●.
   a 330 cm ● $3\frac{1}{4}$ m   b 450 cm ● $4\frac{1}{2}$ m
6. What fraction (part) of each shape is coloured?
   a   b 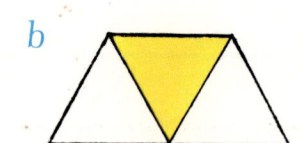   c

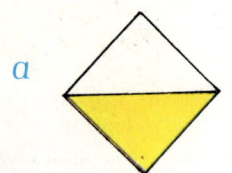

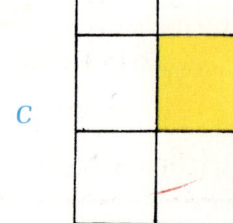

169

1. How many hundreds are there in two thousand?
2. What is the cost of the pencil sharpener?
3. Share 4 fives and 2 twos equally among 3 boys and 3 girls. How much does each child get?
4. What is the distance in kilometres from Ben's home to the sports centre by way of the coach station and library?
5. Write the correct sign (>, < or =) in place of each ◼.
   a 2075 g ◼ $2\frac{3}{4}$ kg   b $1\frac{1}{4}$ kg ◼ 1025 g
6. 1500 g × 4 = ◼ kg

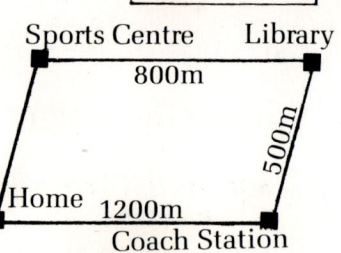

79 seventy-nine

170

1 With 10 spins of the wheel,
  a what is the highest possible score?
  b what is the lowest possible score?
2 List the next five odd numbers greater than 16.
3 157 = ☐ + 17
4 Sue handed a shopkeeper 3 fives and 4 twos for a grapefruit. Sue had a penny change. How much was the grapefruit?
5 A swimming pool is 50 metres long. How many lengths must David swim in a $\frac{1}{2}$-km race?
6 How many kilograms of dog food are there altogether?

171

1 Round off 2062 to the nearest hundred.
2 Write the numerals that are between:
  1199, ☐, ☐, 1202.
3   A Science
    B Travel
    C History

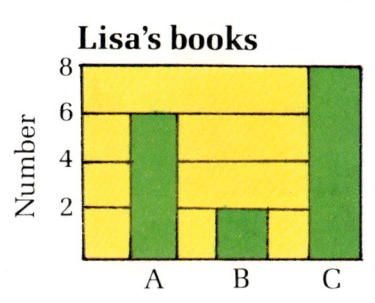

  How many books has Lisa altogether?

4 How many more travel and history books has she than science books?

80 eighty

5 Ali has 63p. How much more does he need to buy 4 apple tarts at 20p each?

6 Name the shapes that are squares.

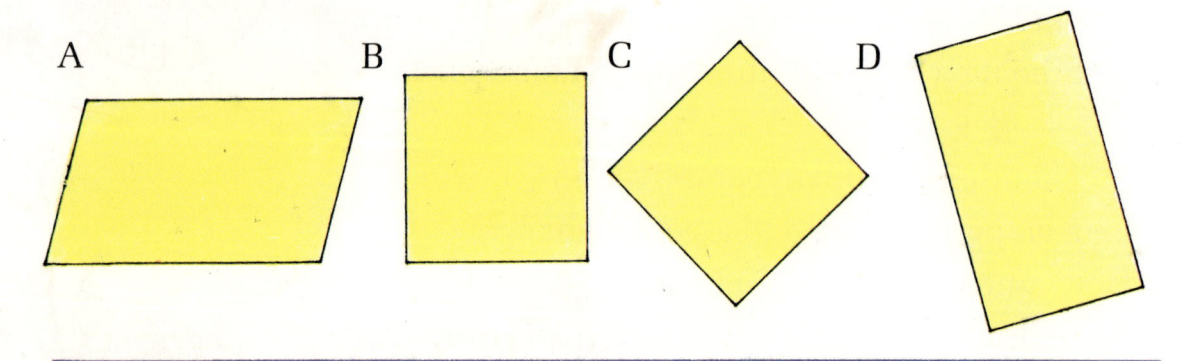

A   B   C   D

172

1 Write the numeral on this calculator in words.

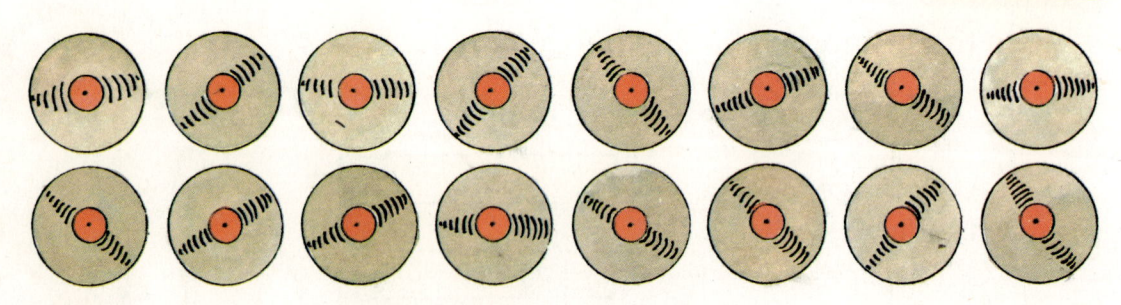

[5005]

2 If these records were arranged in rows with 4 in each row, how many rows would there be?

3 How many batteries can I buy with 4 fifties?

4 Sue Lin had $\frac{1}{2}$ or ▧ sweets.

5 Jane had $\frac{1}{4}$ or ▧ sweets.

6 Peter had the remainder or ▧ sweets.